Copyright for Creatives

Evan M. Butterfield

THIS BOOK DOES NOT CONSTITUTE LEGAL ADVICE. This book is intended to provide accurate information regarding the subject matter covered. It is sold with the understanding that the author, publisher, and distributors are not engaged in rendering legal or other professional services. If legal advice or other expert assistance is required, you should contact a competent professional person.

For Durrell, who puts up with all my nonsense.

Acknowledgments

Thanks to my awesome reviewers, Marie Spodek and Durrell Dew, and to my long-suffering agent, Cynthia Zigmund. Because of them, this book exists and mostly makes sense.

Copyright © 2022 by Evan M. Butterfield. All rights reserved. This work includes public domain material, open access content, and US government documents and publications; no copyright is claimed over that material, identified in the text.

No part of this book may be reproduced or transmitted in any form by any means, electronic or mechanical, including photocopying, recording, or by any other information storage and retrieval system, without the express written permission of the author, except where permitted by law.

ISBN 9798817206722

Before You Start...

Special Features

This book has several special features designed to help you more clearly understand what can sometimes be a tough topic.

Copyright Insights *appear when it's important to emphasize the real-world application of copyright law, showcase tips for how to use copyright law, or highlight best practices.*

©ase Study **Case studies** are summaries of interesting and/or important court decisions, stories, or retelling of actual events that illustrate the concepts being discussed.

License Alert! **License Alerts** let you know when an online platform or other media resource automatically requires you to grant them a license to use your creative content in some way, in exchange for the use of the platform. (These are found mostly in Chapter 9.)

 Four Things. At the end of each chapter in Parts 1 and 3, you'll find a brief review of four key concepts for you to remember about the topic covered.

Commonly-Used Abbreviations

- USC ... US Code, the collection of federal statutes (laws)
- CFR ... Code of Federal Regulations, rules for how the government operates.
- *Id.* ... The citation is the same as the previous footnote

- See, e.g. ... The citation is one example among many
- U.S or S.Ct. ... A US Supreme Court decision
- F.2d or F.3d ... A US Circuit Court of Appeals decision
- F.Supp or F.Supp 2d ... A federal trial court decision

Introduction To Case Citations

A basic citation tells you the name of the case, where it was published and by what court, and the year it was decided. Here's an obviously fictional example:

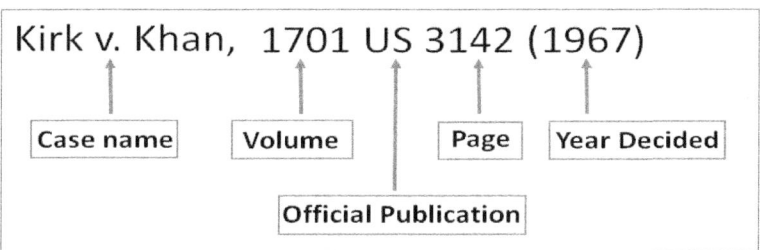

Here, Kirk is the plaintiff (the person who is suing someone[1]) and Khan is the defendant (the person being sued). This is a decision published in the United States Reports, the official publication of US Supreme Court decisions. We know this is probably the last word on a case that was tried, appealed, and then brought to the Supreme Court.

1701 is the volume number of the publication, and 3142 is the page in that volume where the decision starts. The decision was published in 1967—although the original trial was probably many years earlier. Note that in a non-Supreme Court decision, the citation will include the state and/or federal court district along with the year.

OK, I think you're ready to get started now.

---

[1] In a federal civil or criminal case, the plaintiff is always the United States. In private lawsuits the plaintiff and defendant are specific, named persons.

Contents

PART ONE   COPYRIGHT LAW FOR CREATIVES

Chapter 1 What is Copyright? 3

History of copyright
Copyright is Constitutional
Copyright defined
Copyright is a bundle of sticks
How does copyright happen?
Plagiarism and infringement

Chapter 2 What Can't be Copyrighted 19

Copyright v. Trademark v. Patent
What's not protected by copyright
Ideas • Dancing • Recipes and formulas • Fashion and other "useful articles" • Names, titles phrases, and expressions • Facts and common knowledge • Common and geometric shapes • Familiar symbols & designs • Colors • Scènes à faire • Fonts, calligraphy, layout, and blank forms • Naturally occurring materials • Mechanical processes & random selection • Works for hire

Chapter 3 Fair Use & Educational Use 41

Yes but... (Affirmative Defenses)
Credit's not enough
Fair use
Parody
Educational use

PART TWO COPYRIGHT & YOUR CREATIVE WORK

Chapter 4 Crafts 65

Jewelry
Pottery
Stained-glass
Toys
Woodwork

Chapter 5 Graphic Arts 73

Cartoons, comic strips & comic books
Characters
Fan art
Calligraphy
Board games
Graffiti
Graphic design
Tattoos

Chapter 6 Music 87

Musical compositions
Musical performances
Musical recordings
Musical sampling

Chapter 7 Needlework & Clothing 99

Clothing
Costumes
Needlework, fabrics, & quilts
Patterns
Pattern books
Project books
T-shirts

Chapter 8 Performing Arts 115

Comedy
Dance
Performance art
Theater

Chapter 9 Social Media 129

Copyright, licenses, and social media
Facebook
Instagram
OnlyFans
Tiktok
Twitter
YouTube

Chapter 10 Visual Arts 145

Film-making
Fan films
Architecture
Gardening/landscape
Painting and sculpture
Photography

Chapter 11 Technology 167

Computer programs and games
Podcasts
Websites

Chapter 12 Writing 173

Literary works
Fiction
Fan fiction
Nonfiction
Poetry

PART THREE   PROTECT YOUR CREATIVE WORK

Chapter 13 Registering Your Copyright 185

US Copyright Office
Registration: making it official
Registration process
The final decision: register or not?

Chapter 14   Open Access 203

Traditional publishing
Open access
Creative commons
Copyright and creative commons
When licensing isn't enough
Choices

Chapter 15 A Bit About Trademarks 217

What is a trademark?
The Abercrombie categories
Becoming generic
Colors and smells
What can't be trademarked?
Trademark infringement lawsuits

Chapter 16 Introduction to Patents 233

What are patents?
Types of patents
What can be patented
What can't be patented?
How will people know I have a patent?

About the Author/Learn More 243

PART 1

COPYRIGHT LAW

FOR CREATIVES

You might think that "copyright" is a big, monolithic "thing" that you can point to. That you can slap your name or a © on something and that's that.

But it's not, really. Like most things in law (and life) it's not quite that simple. It's nuanced and sometimes complicated and it doesn't always comply with common sense, and that's why you need books like this one.

Before we get started, there are three basic facts you need to know about copyright.

1. It's a **constitutional right**, just like the right to free speech or the right to bear arms.
2. Like any constitutional right, it's not without **rules and limitations** (you can't yell fire in a crowded theater, and we're still trying to figure out exactly what a "well-regulated militia" is).
3. There are **exceptions** to every rule.

In the first three chapters of this book, we'll look at all those things—plus a few more—to help you understand exactly what copyright is, and what it isn't; what it covers and what it doesn't cover; and how you can use it to protect your creative work from being "borrowed" by other people.

You've heard it a million times: "Imitation is the sincerest form of flattery." Well, in the world of creative work, imitation is often the sincerest form of theft. Yes, I said theft. *Your creative work is your property*, and when someone "flatters" you by copying it, they're stealing your property. That's basically the fundamental rule of copyright:

Don't take other people's stuff.

There are three kinds of property in the world, under law. There's **real property**, which includes things like a house or land. There's **personal property**, which is your stuff: things you can touch and things you can't. *Tangible personal property* includes things like your car, your phone, or jewelry. *Intangible personal property* includes things like insurance or stock or money—where the value of the thing is not really in the part you can touch (an insurance policy or cash) but in what it represents: an amount of gold, or the value of a company or help paying hospital bills.[2]

The third type of property is **intellectual property**. Intellectual property doesn't mean your property is smart, or even that the property is owned by an especially smart person (although you are clearly exceptionally intelligent). Intellectual property (IP) is a kind of property that includes things like inventions, writing, and artistic works: things you create with your own imagination, your own creativity, your own hands. You can't copyright real property, and you can't copyright personal property. But copyrights were created precisely to protect intellectual property.

In this book, we're all about your intellectual property: how to protect it, how to protect yourself, and how to avoid violating other people's rights. So let's get started.

---

[2] 41 CFR § 102-36.40

Chapter 1

What is Copyright?

HISTORY OF COPYRIGHT

Let's step back for a moment. In England in 1710—seventy-seven years before the US Constitution was written, Parliament passed the Statute of Queen Anne. From the invention of the printing press in the 15th century, the rights to any books or other printed material belonged to the person who owned the press—that is, *publishers*.

The Statute of Queen Anne was unique, because it established for the first time that there was a fundamental right held by *authors*. Under the Statute, publishers held a total monopoly on the works they published for 14 years from the date of publication. But, the statute said, "after the expiration of the said term of fourteen years, the sole right of printing or disposing of copies shall return to the authors thereof, if they are then living, for another term of fourteen years." In other words, the publisher got a monopoly for 14 years, but then the rights reverted to the author for another 14 years, after which the work became **public domain**—that means that anyone is free to use the work without permission.

What's really important here is that phrase, "the sole right of printing or disposing of copies shall return to the authors." That means the government recognized that the work was "owned" by its author all along, and the publisher's monopoly was more a license than ownership. That was a completely new idea.

COPYRIGHT IS CONSTITUTIONAL

There's a lot to both admire and criticize about the Founding Fathers of the United States, but when it came to copyright, they were positively progressive. The Statute of Queen Anne, as we just saw, granted rights to authors for the first time, but those rights were secondary to the fourteen-years publishers owned the work. The Founders took the concept of author rights and went farther than Queen Anne could ever have imagined.

In the United States, copyright is established in the Constitution, which was written in 1787. Article 1, Section 8, Clause 8 of the Constitution says:

> *The Congress shall have Power...To promote the Progress of Science and the useful Arts, by securing for limited Times to Authors and Inventors the exclusive Right to their respective Writings and Discoveries.*[3]

There are 3 key concepts that underlie US copyright law, as set forth in the Constitution:

1. *To promote Progress*: Copyright law is designed to encourage "progress of Science and the Useful Arts." Science is pretty obvious, but what are "useful arts"? Well, in the 18th century (when the Constitution was written) "useful arts" were things like manufacturing and craftsmanship, mapmaking and shipbuilding—stuff like that. The Founders weren't necessarily thinking much about poetry and music, and certainly weren't thinking about movies, but by the time copyright got put into a statute, and over the course of the centuries since, that brief sentence in the Constitution has been interpreted as referring to pretty much anything that

---

[3] United States Constitution, Article 1 § 8 Clause 8

anyone creates. The significant idea, though, is that the Founders intended that the primary purpose of copyright wasn't to make sure authors got rich, but to promote progress in the new nation.

2. *For limited Times*: Protections are designed to balance the right of creators to profit from their work, but also allow for progress by making things available to everyone at some point.

3. *To Authors and Inventors*: This is important. Before the 18th century, there was really no concept of copyright for authors. If you wrote a book or a play and published it, it was out in the world and anyone could do as they liked with it. If you were lucky enough to have sold it to a publisher, you were paid for that first sale; after that, nothing. If anyone owned your work, it was the publisher.

The Founders Go Further

Back to that phrase in the Constitution, "to Authors and Inventors." What the Founders did was to take the Statute of Queen Anne and turn it on its head (much like they'd done to the British Empire itself a decade earlier). Instead of focusing on publishers' interests, the Constitution gives authors (and inventors) all rights to their work. That was kind of a big deal, at least in the world of copyright.

As usual, the Constitution provides just the broad strokes, though; the details of how copyright law works are found in the US Code, which—unlike the Constitution—is frequently modified and updated by Congress in response to court decisions, technology changes, and pressure from the public and special interests.

The copyright privileges that Congress has created are not designed to provide a special private benefit. Rather, copyright is seen as "a means by which an important public purpose may be achieved. It is intended to motivate the creative activity of authors and inventors by the provision of a special reward, and to allow the public access to the products of their genius after the limited period of exclusive control has expired."[4]

"The limited scope of the copyright holder's statutory monopoly, like the limited copyright duration required by the Constitution, reflects a balance of competing claims upon the public interest: Creative work is to be encouraged and rewarded, but private motivation must ultimately serve the cause of promoting broad public availability of literature, music, and the other arts. The immediate effect of our copyright law is to secure a fair return for [a creator's] creative labor. But the ultimate aim is, by this incentive, to stimulate artistic creativity for the general public good. The sole interest of the United States and the primary object in conferring the monopoly...lie[s] in the general benefits derived by the public from the labors of [creators]."[5]

COPYRIGHT DEFINED

"Copyright" is best defined as "A collection of legally-defined exclusive rights held by the creator of original content for a limited period of time." Simple enough, right? Well, let's break that definition down a bit and see what it actually means.

"A collection of legally-defined exclusive rights..."

To start with, copyright isn't a right, it's a *collection* of rights. Based on statute and case law, there are five basic, fundamental rights that a copyright holder owns. They are:

1. The right to *publish* your content—and remember that "publish" literally means "to distribute publicly"— it's not limited to a book or magazine article.
2. The right to *adapt* your content, to make changes to it

---

[4] *Sony Corp. of America v Universal City Studios, Inc.,* 464 US 417 (1984)
[5] *Twentieth Century Music Corp. v. Aiken*, 422 US 151, 156 (1975)

3. The right to *perform* it—read it, dance it, sing it, whatever
4. The right to *display* it – to show it to other people publicly
5. The right to *reproduce* it: make and distribute copies

COPYRIGHT IS A BUNDLE OF STICKS

The easiest way to think about this collection of rights is as a bundle of sticks. This is a bundle of sticks:

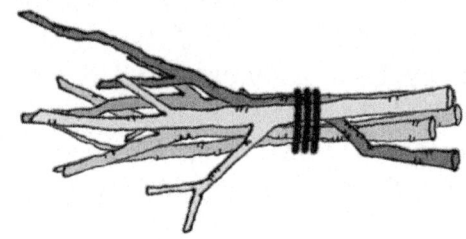

Each stick in that bundle represents one of the five copyright rights:

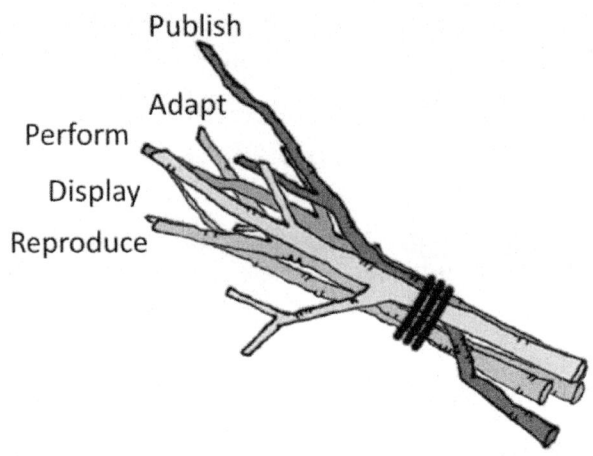

So let's unbundle those sticks and see what those rights are.

Right to Publish

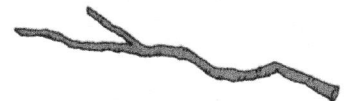

The right to publish means that the copyright holder is the only person who can publish or distribute the work by sale, rental, lease, lending, or give it away for free.

It's important to note, though, that the copyright holder only controls the *first distribution* of a particular copy of his or her work. This is known as the **First Sale Doctrine**.

Under the First Sale Doctrine, once a copy of copyrighted work has been sold to a consumer, the author/creator has no control over how that copy is used or distributed—as long as none of the other rights are infringed. Remember, this refers to any copyrightable work: a book or magazine article, a song or painting or movie or sculpture—any work that meets the requirements for copyright.

For example, if someone writes a book, they own the copyright, and can decide who if anyone gets to sell it on their behalf, such as a publisher or distributor. But if a book is self-published, then the author can decide who to sell it to on an individual basis, and even refuse to sell it to someone. Once it's been sold, the author still holds the copyright, but no longer has any control over what happens to that copy of her book. So once you buy the book, you're free to resell it, or turn it into a planter, or give it away, or tear out all the pages to make a flock of origami birds. The point is, the author has no control over what you do with their book (or any other copyrightable work) once you've bought it.[6]

But what you *can't* do is claim that you wrote the book, or take its characters and plot and make your own book or movie based on them, or reproduce the book and sell copies—in other words, the buyer has complete control over what's done with the *one*

---

[6] In Chapter 10, we'll meet at an exception to this rule, under the Visual Artists Rights Act (VARA) of 1990.

single copy they paid for, and no more. If the buyer infringes on any of the author's sticks, the author can fight back in the courts for infringement.

And remember: while this example of the First Sale Doctrine focuses on books, the doctrine—and copyright generally—applies to a wide range of other creative work...as we'll see in Part Two.

CASE STUDY A group of investors purchased a rare book—a copy of the late Chilean-French experimental filmmaker Alejandro Jodorowsky's detailed plans, production notes, and illustrations for a never-made 1970s movie based on Frank Herbert's novel, *Dune*. They paid roughly $3 million for the book. The group then released a "manifesto" on Twitter declaring their intent to "make the book public," and "produce an original animated limited series inspired by the book and sell it to a streaming service."

You should be able to see immediately what the problem is here. The group won *a copy* of the book at auction, not any of the rights to it. As purchasers of Jodorowsky's *Dune* they are absolutely entitled to read it, show it to other people, or make its pages into origami birds. What they can't do with it (as you should now know) is make the book public, create an animated series based it, or support any derivative uses of it created by other people. Not only don't they have rights to Jodorowsky's *Dune*, they don't have rights to Herbert's novels, on which the book and proposed movie are based. [7]

Right to Adapt

The next stick in the copyright holder's bundle is the right to adapt the work. Only the copyright holder has the right to make

---

[7] See, e.g., Ongweso, E., "SpiceDAO Roasted for Spending $3.8 Million on Jodorowsky's 'Dune' Book." Vice.com (January 18, 2022)

any adaptation of the work, referred to as a **derivative work** because it's *derived* from the original.

A "derivative work" is a transformational work based on one or more preexisting original works, such as a:
- Translation
- Musical arrangement
- Dramatization
- Fictionalization
- Movie version
- Sound recording
- Representation in another artistic medium
- Condensed or abridged version

So only the copyright holder has the right to create or approve the creation of derivative content—content derived from the original material. If the author licenses someone to create a translation, or an annotated edition, the added content may be copyrightable by the new creator, but the core content still belongs to the original creator.

However, people other than the copyright holder are allowed to make **transformative works** based on the original without permission.

"Transformative" means the copyrighted material was used in a way that the resulting new work is fully copyrightable on its own. There are strict rules about transformative use (which we'll discuss in the next chapter), but a good example of a transformative use is a parody: the original work is recognizable—it has to be for the parody to be funny—but the creator of the parody has transformed the original work into something that's new and stands on its own as an artistic statement. Turning the pages of a book into a flock of origami birds would absolutely be transformative.

CASE STUDY A good example of a transformative work is a book written in 2001 by author Alice Randall, called *The Wind Done Gone*. The novel is a parody of Margaret Mitchell's 1936 novel, *Gone With The Wind*, in which the characters and story of Mitchell's novel are described and commented on by a narrator who is a slave on Scarlett O'Hara's plantation. The Mitchell Estate sued Randall for copyright infringement, and Randall successfully argued that her work was transformative: it cast the story and characters of Mitchell's novel, which painted a romantic and flattering picture of the South before the Civil War, in a more historically realistic light.[8]

Other popular examples of solid transformative work in which the original is recognizable are the song parodies Weird Al Yankovic and Randy Rainbow. While Weird Al routinely asks for permission from the musicians whose work he parodies, the concept of transformative work means he's being polite, but he doesn't have to ask.

Right to Perform

The next stick in the bundle of rights is the right to perform. Only the copyright holder has the right to control the public performance of certain types of works:

- Literary works
- Musical works
- Dramatic works
- Choreography
- Pantomimes
- Motion pictures
- Audio/visual works

---

[8] *Suntrust Bank v. Houghton Mifflin Co.*, 136 FSupp 2d 1357 (ND Ga., 2001)

A "public performance" is when the work is performed in a "place open to the public or at a place where a substantial number of persons outside of a normal circle of a family and its social acquaintances are gathered,"[9] or transmitted to multiple locations via such media as television, Internet, and radio.

Right to Reproduce

The next stick is the right to **reproduce** the work.

Only the copyright owner has the right to make any reproductions or copies of the work.

Reproduction includes:

- Photocopying printed material
- Duplicating software
- Copying text
- Sampling music

It doesn't matter how much of the work is copied by someone who's not authorized by the copyright holder: all the law requires to find infringement is that the copying was substantial and material.

Right to Display

Finally, the last stick in the copyright holder's bundle is the right to **display** the work. Only the copyright holder has the right to display the work in public.

This right is limited to the following types of works:

---

[9] 17 USC §101

Literary	Pictorial
Musical	Graphical
Dramatic	Sculptural
Choreographic	Still images from motion pictures/audio/video
Pantomimes	

"...held by the creator of original content..."

The next element is that the rights are held by the creator of **original content**. "Original content" is pretty much what it suggests: content that is new and unique.

Original content can be based on or derived from other existing content, if the result is something that's "new and unique"—that is, sufficiently transformed from the original so as to not be infringing.

Something that's new and unique obviously can't be an exact duplication of any part of a prior work. But it doesn't have to be useful or even of good quality: a bad song is just as copyrightable as a good one, as long as it's original. Copyright doesn't give two hoots whether your work is any good or not, as long as it's new and original.

"...for a limited period of time."

Finally, the definition states that the collection of rights is held by the creator for a limited period of time. This is the really important piece of the definition of copyright.

What constitutes a "limited period of time" has varied over time, but currently, copyright lasts for the life of the creator plus 70 years, which means the standard copyright period is more or less 150 years or so, depending on the health of the author. Note that the copyright period is measured by the creator's life, not the date of publication. The date of publication has nothing to do with your calculation of how long copyright will last. If the work is a joint work with multiple authors, the term lasts for 70 years after the last surviving author's death.

For works published between 1923 and 1977, copyright is in force for 95 years from the year of first publication. Works published before 1923 are generally in the public domain. Be careful, though: specific versions of works may remain protected. For instance, author A. A. Milne's book, Winnie-the-Pooh *became public domain in 2022, but the* Disney *version of Pooh, licensed & created in 1961, is still protected.*

Public Domain

"Public Domain" literally means creative materials that are not protected by intellectual property laws. The *public* owns these works, not an individual author or artist. Anyone can use a public domain work without obtaining permission, but no one can ever own public domain work exclusively. Some works become public domain due to age, and some—like works published by the government—are public domain from the beginning. Other works can become public domain because their creators want their work to be freely available. (We'll see that in Chapter 14.)

HOW DOES COPYRIGHT HAPPEN?

Copyright exists **automatically** in any original work of authorship once it is fixed in a tangible medium. You literally don't have to do anything to copyright your work: by creating it in a tangible medium, and showing it to others, you've done all you need to do to have a copyright. The tricky part is that to have an enforceable copyright—that is, something that allows you to take an infringer to court and collect damages—requires registration with the Copyright Office.

There is no such thing as a "poor man's copyright." Mailing yourself a copy of your work has zero effect on its copyright status, and just wastes postage. Don't bother.[10]

What About the © ?

Applying a copyright notice to a work has not been required since March 1, 1989, but it still provides some practical and legal benefits. For example, a copyright notice:

- Identifies the copyright owner at the time of first publication for parties seeking permission to use the work.
- Identifies the year of first publication, which can be used to determine the term of copyright for anonymous or pseudonymous works or works made for hire.
- May prevent the work from becoming an "orphan" by identifying the copyright owner or specifying the term of copyright. ("Orphan works" are original works of authorship for which prospective users cannot identify or locate copyright owners to request permission.)

However, placing a copyright notice on a work is *not* a substitute for registration. As we'll see in Chapter 13, there are a lot of compelling reasons for registering a copyright with the United States Copyright Office.

PLAGIARISM AND INFRINGEMENT

This is as good a place as any to point out that plagiarism is not the same thing as copyright infringement. Plagiarism is a vague kind of stealing of another's literary work, but copyright infringement—as we've seen--has a strict legal definition.

Copyright infringement can occur even if exact lines are not literally copied. Copying and modifying lines can be

---

[10] US Copyright Office, FAQs https://www.copyright.gov/help/faq/faq-general.html

infringement because derivative works are protected by copyright. Also, nonliteral infringement can occur when the organization of scenes or chapters are identical even if the words are not identical.

Plagiarism is generally broader than copyright infringement and has no strict legal definition. Copyrights protect the expression of ideas but not the ideas themselves, whereas plagiarism can encompass the theft of ideas. If you write a great new script for a superhero movie about a man who can climb walls and shoot sticky webs from his wrists, you may be accused of the ethical misconduct called plagiarism, but not necessarily the legal misconduct called copyright infringement. However, if you copy exact dialog out of the Spider-Man screenplay, then you have probably crossed the line into copyright infringement.

A plagiarist may also be violating copyright, or may not be, but the offense isn't dependent on the status of what's been copied. You can plagiarize a work that's public domain the same as you can plagiarize something that's under copyright. And while you won't go to jail for plagiarism per se there are still consequences.[11] Those consequences include, for students, failing a class or even being expelled. For professionals, having plagiarism discovered is absolutely embarrassing, can result in firing, will certainly cloud a professional reputation, and can result in the plagiarist being sued by the copyright holder or other injured party.

---

[11] As we'll see, you *can* go to jail for copyright infringement, and plagiarism is obviously a flavor of copyright infringement.

 **So what do you take away from all this? Here are four key points to remember:**

1. Copyright is in the United States Constitution, right along with freedom of speech and the right to vote. So it's important.
2. Copyright isn't just one right, it's a bunch of rights that copyright holders can do anything they want to with.
3. Copyright may not be forever, but it *is* for a very, very, very long time. "Life of the creator plus 70 years" is the general rule.
4. Like other things, copyright happens. You don't need to do anything special to copyright what you've created: as long as what you've made *can* be copyrighted, it automatically *is* copyrighted. But there are some things you can do to make your copyright stronger and more effective.

Chapter 2
What's Not Protected?

As we saw in Chapter 1, to be copyrightable something has meet two basic requirements:

1. The creation must be in a fixed, tangible medium of expression that can be seen, reproduced, or recorded; and
2. The creation must be published.

Now, "published" is not a word that's limited to books or magazine articles; in copyright law, the word means that the work was *made available to the public* ("public-ation") on an unrestricted basis. "Publication" includes public performances and posting on the Internet, not just something printed and distributed by a publisher. But if a limitation is placed on distribution, then the work is not published for purposes of copyright law.

What that means is this: If you write a poem or paint a picture, and then hide it away in a locked drawer and throw the key in a river, you haven't met the copyright requirements. Someday, when someone smashes that drawer open, your work isn't protected by copyright law. You created it, and it's in a fixed medium, but it was never published, so too bad.

Copyright law talks about "authors" and "authorship" a lot, but what that word means in copyright law is not limited to writers: it means anyone who creates something copyrightable. So painters, photographers, sculptors, composers—they're all "authors" under copyright law.

COPYRIGHT v. TRADEMARK v. PATENT

In a moment, we'll look at each of those unprotected things individually, plus some other types of creative work generally not protectable by copyright. But first, let's quickly address that while this book is primarily about protecting your creative work through copyright, there are in fact three different ways that creative people can protect their stuff. If copyright doesn't work for you, it's possible that trademark or patent law provides a safety net.

We'll consider trademarks and patents briefly in later chapters, but for now here's a quick overview of the three types of protection:

Copyright

What's Protected? Artistic, literary, or intellectually created works, such as novels, music, movies, software code, photographs, and paintings that are original and exist in a tangible medium, such as paper, canvas, film, or digital format. For example, the song lyrics to "Let It Go" from the movie, *Frozen*.

What's the Benefit? Protects your exclusive right to reproduce, distribute, and perform or display the created work, and prevents other people from copying or exploiting the creation without your permission, for a period of your life plus 70 years.

Trademark[12]

What's Protected? A word, phrase, design, or combination that identifies your goods or services, distinguishes them from the goods or services of others, and indicates the source of your goods or services. For example, the Nike swoosh.

What's the Benefit? Protects the trademark from being registered by others without your permission and helps you prevent others from using a trademark that is similar to yours, with similar goods or services, for indefinitely renewable periods of 10 years.

Patent[13]

What's Protected? Technical inventions, such as chemical compositions like pharmaceutical drugs, mechanical processes like machinery, or machine designs that are new, unique, and usable in some type of industry, like a new type of hybrid car engine.

What's the Benefit? Protects your right to manufacture, sell, and distribute your invention, and prevents others from copying, or making, using or selling the invention without your consent, for a period of 20 years.

For example, Coca-Cola holds copyrights on the artwork and text in its ads (like the iconic Santa Claus or polar bears, or the lyrics to "I'd Like to Teach the World to Sing"). Coca-Cola holds trademarks on its logos, and patents on its formula and bottle shape.

WHAT'S <u>NOT</u> PROTECTED BY COPYRIGHT?

To understand copyright law, it's important to understand the requirements for something to be copyrighted. It's also

---

[12] See Chapter 15
[13] See Chapter 16

important to understand that not every creative work can be copyrighted at all. Copyright is not without its limits.

The following is the traditional list of creative efforts that are, under law, specifically *not* protectible by copyright:[14]

- Ideas
- Choreography
- Recipes and Formulas
- Fashion
- Names, Titles, Short Phrases, or Expressions
- Facts and Commonly Known Information

Those exclusions are actually a good thing: they helpfully allow us to wear clothes and observe that the sky is blue, and call each other by our names, and eat, and dance like no one's watching without having to pay someone royalties.

Ideas

Copyright only protects things that are in a "fixed and tangible" form. That is, things that can be presented to others. Ideas can't be copyrighted, because an idea is nothing more than electrons flying around between synapses in your brain. However, the "expression" of an idea *can* be copyrighted. In other words, you can't copyright the idea for your novel, but your novel is absolutely copyrightable.

The Copyright Act is clear: "In no case does copyright protection for an original work of authorship extend to any idea, procedure, process, system, method of operation, concept, principle, or discovery, regardless of the form in which it is described, explained, illustrated, or embodied in such work."[15] Once an idea is fixed in a tangible form of expression, though, it's protectible.

---

[14] US Copyright Office, *Circular 33: Works Not Protected by Copyright* (rev'd 2021)
[15] 17 USC § 102(b)

Ideas aren't protectible by copyright, because they are intangible; they exist only in your mind. Even if you write your idea down (so it's "tangible"), the only way it's copyrightable is if it's the complete manifestation of your concept. Writing the phrase "a novel about 19th century pirates who ride in steam-powered blimps" won't do the trick. You actually have to write the novel *Sky Pirates!* and then copyright that. (And if you do, I'll probably read it!)

The key here is that just having an idea doesn't make it a thing: you need to actually take steps to create something that's tangible—that's the "property" part of "intellectual property."

Choreography and Dance*

Choreographic works are *only* protected if they're recorded somehow—in choreographic notation, for instance, or video. Just doing a dance doesn't make it intellectual property (particularly when *I* do a dance).

The Copyright Office lists three acceptable formats for the fixation of choreographic works:

- Dance notation, Such as Benesh Dance Notation
- Video recordings of a performance
- Textual descriptions, photographs, or drawings[16]

However, common movements or activities, like yoga positions, line dances and exercise routines, are not copyrightable, even when they are unique. Individual ballet or dance positions that are commonly used are also not copyrightable, because they're commonly-used and not unique.

---

[16] *Id.*
* See Part Two

Recipes and Formulas*

A simple list of ingredients is not protected under copyright law. However, where a recipe or formula is accompanied by "substantial literary expression in the form of an explanation or directions, or when there is a collection of recipes as in a cookbook," it may be possible to protect the content. [17]

> *If you have secret ingredients in a recipe that you don't want everyone to know about, you should not submit your recipe for registration, because applications and deposit copies become searchable public records.*

That means that recipes (and other formulas) can't be copyrighted, because at their core they are simply lists of items and quantities, and copyright does not protect facts; facts belong to everyone.[18]

Now, that's not to say that a book of recipes *can't* be copyrighted (Betty Crocker and Fannie Farmer would be alarmed if that were true). But in that case what's protected is the *collection* of recipes, the layout, the design, and the narrative instructions and descriptions of the baking process—if those instructions are unique and not just a simple list of steps.

The list of ingredients and basic instructions for combining them cannot receive a copyright, but whatever the maker has added creatively to the process is.[19] In other words, a recipe that creatively explains how to perform a particular part of the process may be copyrightable, as are any photographs or illustrations created (or owned) by the author.[20] If a baker

---

[17] US Copyright Office, *Circular 33: Works Not Protected by Copyright* (rev'd 2021)
[18] *Id.*
[19] See, e.g., *Tomaydo-Tomahhdo, L.L.C. v. Vozary*, 629 Fed.Appx. 658, 661 (6th Cir.2015).
[20] US Copyright Office, Circular 33: *Works Not Protected by Copyright* (rev'd 2021)

produced recipes and instructions in the form of a sonnet, however, she could probably copyright them.[21]

Fashion and Other "Useful Articles"*

Clothing is considered a "useful article" under US copyright law. Unfortunately, copyright law does not protect "useful articles." Under the Copyright Act, a useful article is "an article having an intrinsic utilitarian function that is not merely to portray the appearance of the article or to convey information."[22] Useful articles include things like machinery and tools; medical instruments; household appliances, fixtures, and furniture; and fabrics and clothing.[23] Other examples of potentially "useful articles" provided in statute are maps, globes, charts, diagrams, models, and technical drawings, including architectural plans."[24]

Note that while copyright *won't protect "useful articles,"* usefulness *is one of the requirements for a patent.*

However, any *parts* of useful articles that are creative and can be separated from the useful object's function may be protected by copyright.[25]

So, for instance, a woodworker could build a beautiful coatrack, but it's still a functional coatrack so it can't be copyrighted. However, if the carpenter uses a wood burner to inscribe an original poem onto the coatrack, the poem is copyrightable, just not the thing it's carved into.

---

[21] See Chapter 12.
* See Part Two
[22] 17 USC § 101
[23] US Copyright Office, *Compendium* of US Copyright Office Practices, Third Edition (Section 924.1)
[24] 17 USC § 101, "Pictorial, graphic, and sculptural works"
[25] US Copyright Office, *Compendium* of US Copyright Office Practices, Third Edition (§ 906.10)

There's a carve-out in this general rule, though, for things that are works of "artistic craftsmanship." Artistic craftsmanship means "works of artistic craftsmanship insofar as their form but not their mechanical or utilitarian aspects are concerned."[26] Basically, all that means is that the object has the functionality of a useful article, but its design and execution are purely artistic in nature.

In other words, a thing is a "useful article" if it primarily serves a mechanical or utilitarian function, even if it has some elements of artistic craftsmanship.

To go back to our coatrack, imagine that the woodworker didn't simply build a panel with some hooks to hang coats on, but rather carved an elaborate, curving, interwoven object that looks like something from Dr Seuss. It's still something to hang a coat on, but its functional purpose is now secondary to its aesthetic value; it's a work of artistic craftsmanship, and may be protected by copyright.

Clothing*

We've established that clothing is a useful article under copyright law, which is probably a good thing for the general modesty of society. But as with all things in the law, there are some exceptions and special circumstances of interest to people who make clothing.

For instance, a dress *pattern* could be considered artistic, since it is essentially a drawing of something and therefore an original creative work. But the thing it's a drawing of—a shirt or dress—serves the useful function of not having everyone wander around naked, and so it can't be copyrighted.

This can get confusing, so let's break it down a little bit more.

---

[26] *Id.*, at § 925.1; see Chapter 10, Visual Arts
* See Part Two

A dress *pattern* can be copyrighted, but the way fabric is cut cannot be. A *print* applied to a fabric can be copyrighted, but the fabric itself cannot be—unless the way it's woven, for instance, is particularly unique or creative.[27]

> There are other ways to protect fashion items beyond copyright: trademark may offer protection for colors in some cases, for instance, or design patents can protect an otherwise useful article.

Names, Titles, Phrases and Expressions

The purpose of copyright law is to protect **original works of authorship**—books, paintings, musical compositions, and other artistic or creative expressions. Copyright law doesn't concern itself with personal or business names, titles, short phrases, or common knowledge.[28] Some of those things—names, titles, and phrases—may be protected by trademark law, however.

Names

Fortunately for all of us, we can't copyright our names. The Copyright Office helpfully provides a list[29] of what they won't cover:

- The name of an individual (actual, pen, or stage names)
- The title or subtitle of a work, such as a book, a song, or a pictorial, graphic, or sculptural work
- The name of a business or organization
- The name of a band or performing group
- The name of a product or service
- A domain name or URL
- The name of a character

---

* See Part Two
[27] We'll discuss clothing, costumes, and patterns in detail in Chapter 4.
[28] 37 CFR § 202.1, "Material not subject to copyright"
[29] US Copyright Office, Circular 33: Works Not Protected by Copyright

> As is the case with fashion items, the trademark process may be a better alternative for those wishing to protect names. Kim Kardashian, for example, has trademarked the names of her children—North, Saint, Chicago, and Psalm. Trademark registration requires some specificity about what uses the mark will be put to, and Kardashian included "hair accessories, calendars, books, photo albums, jewelry, handbags, linens, baby bottles, toys, advertising services, skincare products, furniture, clothing, and ... nutritional supplements."

Titles

Similarly, the titles of works are not copyrightable, either. So yes, that means that you can write a book called *Gone With the Wind*, and as long as it doesn't involve misty-eyed nostalgia for slavery and a romanticized retelling of American history and the Civil War, you're good to go. While the content of a book is copyrightable its title is not. What you need to avoid, though, is confusing people about what book they're buying.

Again, trademark may offer an alternative. While the general rule is that book titles cannot be trademarked—because the purpose of a trademark is to identify the source of goods or services, and to distinguish them from other, similar sources—in the case of a title for a book series, the Patent & Trademark Office may permit a book's title to be protected. For instance, the "For Dummies" series published by Wiley is trademarked as a series. If someone wrote a nine-book series chronicling the time-traveling adventures of a pair of cat detectives, an individual book title, like *Muffy & Fluffy and the Fall of the Roman Empire* could not be trademarked. But the series title, *Muffy & Fluffy's Adventures in Time*, referring to the entire series, could be.[30]

---

[30] See Chapter 15 for a brief introductory overview of trademark law.

Short Phrases or Expressions

The Copyright Office is pretty clear on this point:

> To be entitled to copyright protection, a work must contain something capable of being copyrighted — that is, an appreciable amount of original text or pictorial material .... Brand names, trade names, slogans, and other short phrases or expressions cannot be copyrighted, even if they are distinctively arranged or printed.[31]

Specifically, the Copyright Office says that "catchwords or catchphrases, and mottos, slogans, or other short expressions" are ineligible for copyright protection.[32]

So much for copyrighting Homer Simpson's "d'oh!" or "Make America Great Again"—both of which, however, *are* protected as registered trademarks.

Facts and Common Knowledge

Finally, facts can't be copyrighted. The Copyright Office says "facts are not copyrightable and cannot be registered with the US Copyright Office."[33] A person who finds and records a particular fact has not created it; they simply discovered that it was there.[34] "No one may claim originality as to facts ... because facts do not owe their origin to an act of authorship; this is true of all facts—scientific, historical, biographical, and news of the day.'"[35] For the same reason, theories, predictions, or

---

[31] US Copyright Office, *Circular No. 46: Copyright in Commercial Prints and Labels*, cited in *Southco, Inc. v Kanebridge Corp.*, 390 F.3d 276 (3rd Cir., 2004)

[32] US Copyright Office, Circular 33: Works Not Protected by Copyright

[33] US Copyright Office, *Compendium* § 313.3(c)

[34] *Id.*

[35] *Id.*, citing *Feist Publications, Inc. v. Rural Telephone Service Co., Inc.*, 499 US 340 (1991)

conclusions that are asserted to be facts are uncopyrightable, even if the assertion of fact is erroneous or incorrect.[36]

In other words, once you call something a fact, you can't copyright it, even if you're wrong.

For example, newspaper articles are copyrighted, but the copyright doesn't include the facts of the events that occurred, because the journalist didn't create them: they are independent facts that happened. So a news report about an automobile accident can be copyrighted because it contains original descriptions and analysis and interviews; but the fact that the automobile accident occurred doesn't belong to the newspaper.

Common Geometric Shapes

The Copyright Act does not protect common geometric shapes—things like circles, ovals, spheres, triangles, cones, squares, pentagons, hexagons, and octagons.[37] Of course there's an exception: If "the author's use of those shapes results in a work that, as a whole, is sufficiently creative," then it may be copyrightable.

The Copyright Office itself provides some helpful examples of this distinction:[38]

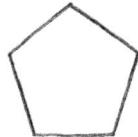
A simple line-drawing of a standard pentagon on a bare white sheet of paper: the Copyright Office will not register the drawing because it consists only of a simple geometric shape.

---

[36] *Id.*
[37] US Copyright Office, *Compendium* of US Copyright Office Practices, Third Edition (Section 906.1).
[38] *Id.* Illustrations by the author

An artist sculpts a perfectly smooth granite sphere: the Copyright Office will not register this work because it is still a common geometric shape, and any pattern or coloring is just the natural stone, rather than the result of creative human expression.

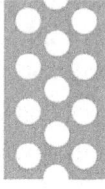
An artist paints a picture with a gray background and evenly spaced white circles: the painting cannot be copyrighted because it features simple geometric symbols, and neither the placement of the circles or rectangle show sufficient original creativity.

A designer creates a giftwrap design that includes various shapes arranged in a random pattern, with each shape a different color: the Copyright Office *will* register the design because it combines various different shapes and colors in an original and creative way.[39]

Familiar Symbols and Designs

Familiar symbols and designs, or unique treatments of familiar symbols and designs, are not protected by the Copyright Act. Like geometric shapes, however, a work that includes familiar symbols or designs may be copyrightable if the familiar symbol or design is used "in a creative manner" and the whole work is eligible for copyright.

Once again, the Copyright Office provides us with some helpful examples:[40]

---

[39] *Id.*
[40] US Copyright Office, Circular 33: Works Not Protected by Copyright

1. An artist creates a sketch of the standard *fleur de lys* design used by the French monarchy. The Copyright Office will likely refuse to register a copyright, because the work merely depicts a familiar symbol.

Standard fleur de lys design. Source: Wikimedia Commons, public domain.

2. Another artist draws an original portrait of Marie Antoinette against a backdrop of multiple *fleur de lys* designs: the Copyright Office will probably approve copyright for this image, because the original, artistic portrait is the focus, and the standard *fleur de lys* designs are merely decorative background for the creative work.

The Copyright Office also provides a helpful list of examples of familiar symbols and designs that can't be copyrighted:

- Letters, punctuation, or symbols on a keyboard
- Abbreviations
- Musical notation
- Numbers and mathematical and currency symbols
- Arrows and other directional or navigational symbols
- Common symbols and shapes, such as a spade, club, heart, diamond, star, yin yang, or (as we saw) fleur de lys
- Common patterns, such as polka dot or checkerboard
- Well-known and commonly used symbols that contain a minimal amount of expression or are in the public domain, such as the peace symbol, gender symbols, or simple emoticons
- Industry designs, such as the caduceus, barber pole, food labeling symbols, or hazard warning symbols
- Familiar religious symbols
- Common architecture moldings[41]

---

[41] US Copyright Office, Circular 33: Works Not Protected by Copyright

Colors

As a rule, colors cannot be copyrighted.[42] It doesn't matter what media is used (paint, computer, or whatever), or whether or not the color or combination of colors is aesthetically pleasing; colors aren't copyrightable. Simply adding color to a basic design is also insufficient for copyright.[43]

However, adding color to a black and white photograph, either through digital tools or with paint or overlays, has been approved by the Copyright Office. That's because adding the colors to an existing work demonstrates sufficient creativity.

You should note that, once again, while copyright is not the answer to your desire to protect a color, trademark may be.[44]

Scènes à faire

Scènes à faire roughly translates as "scenes that must be done." In copyright law, *scènes à faire* is a fancy French way of saying that there is no copyright protection for those features of a work that are indispensable or standard for similar works in the same genre.

Because "[t]he entire dramatic literature of the world can be reduced to some three dozen situations,"[45] it's important that no one is able to monopolize the idea of a story about aliens invading earth, or star-crossed lovers from rival families, or cowboys in the Old West, or soldiers in wartime. If someone could copyright "stories about people flying around in spaceships meeting aliens" it would be hard for *Star Wars* or *Star Trek* to get made.

---

[42] 37 CFR § 202.1(a)
[43] Copyright Registration for Colorized Versions of Black and White Motion Pictures, 52 Fed. Reg. 23,443, 23,444 (June 22, 1987)
[44] See Chapter 15.
[45] *Echevarria v. Warner Bros. Pictures*, 12 F. Supp. 632 (S.D. Cal. 1935)

The exact way those stories are told—the words written, the specific situations, the characters—all those can be copyrighted of course, or in some cases trademarked, but E.L. James (author of the *Shades of Grey* novels) doesn't get to sue another author for writing a novel about romance in the BDSM community. A science fiction novel may involve interstellar travel, aliens from another planet, a heroic starship captain, and the Earth in peril. That author can't sue another science fiction writer for writing a novel involving interstellar travel, aliens from another planet, a heroic starship captain, and the Earth in peril—those are all *scènes à faire*: things and situations a reader will expect in a science fiction novel.

Remember that the Constitution says that copyright (and patent) are established for the *encouragement* of the useful arts, not to wall off a whole genre once someone has produced a work. Heroic starship captains, the Earth in peril, aliens from another planet—these are all elements of a good science fiction story, and no one gets to keep other people from using them.

In short, the *scènes à faire* doctrine prevents monopolies and encourages creative efforts. And that's the goal of copyright, as we already know: the balancing of freedom of expression and the protection of creativity. The doctrine balances the rights of artists to protect their work with an individual's right to create works that address the same theme that others have used in the past.

Fonts, Calligraphy, Layout, and Blank Forms

As a general rule, typeface, fonts, lettering, and calligraphy are not copyrightable.[46] It doesn't matter how unique or creative or fancy your lettering is; if it's just lettering it's not protectable by copyright. The *words* certainly may be, but the lettering isn't.[47]

---

[46] 37 CFR § 202.1(a), (e).
[47] See Chapter 6

Spatial Format and Layout Design

While the layout or design of a book, page, website, or poster is important, it's generally not something that can be protected by copyright. In the same way that a blank form isn't protectable because it's just a "shell" for content, the Copyright Office views page format, layout, and design as a container for the author's content.[48]

Blank Forms

Because blank forms are designed for recording information and don't convey information, they aren't copyrightable.[49]

"Blank forms" is pretty self-explanatory, but it means things like time cards, diaries, bank checks, scorecards, address books, and order forms. Blank forms are not copyrightable for two reasons: first (as mentioned) because they don't convey information, and second because they are really "containers" or "shells" into which copyrightable content *might* be poured. Because simple instructions aren't copyrightable, text labels on a blank form explaining would also not be protectable by copyright. However, if someone adds original, unique content to forms—such as decorative artwork or instructions on how to fill out the form—that content may be copyrightable. Likewise, the Office will refuse to register claims based solely on the arrangement, spacing, or juxtaposition of standard text on a blank form.[50]

This is as good a place as any to point out, though, that sometimes adding copyrightable content to non-copyrightable things results in something that's copyrightable. For instance, court decisions are generally not copyrighted, because they (like other government publications) are in the public domain. But

---

[48] US Copyright Office, *Compendium* of US Copyright Office Practices, Third Edition (Section 906.5)

[49] 37 CFR § 202.1(c)

[50] Registration of Claims to Copyright; Notice of Termination of Inquiry Regarding Blank Forms, 45 Fed. Reg. 63,298 (Sept. 24, 1980)

there are many law book publishers who compile those decisions in volumes, adding summaries, notes, and analysis. The resulting books containing that public domain content are absolutely copyrightable by the publishers, because of the original "literary" content they've added. Because the analysis and notes theoretically make the decision more useful to lawyers, the publisher have added value and created a new work from the public domain content.

Naturally Occurring Materials

Remember that human authorship is one of the basic requirements for copyright protection. As a result, naturally occurring objects, or things found in nature, cannot be copyrighted, because a human didn't create them. This distinction is important for some artists to be aware of, because it doesn't matter that you varnished and mounted the piece of driftwood you found, or that you polished a rock to a silky luster; if it is essentially a natural object, it won't be copyrighted.

Mechanical Processes & Random Selection

Because copyright law only protects works that human beings have created, works that are machine-generated or made with automated processes may not be copyrighted. That means, for instance, that posters created by an automated printing press run by an artificial intelligence using a randomized algorithm would not be protected by copyright. (The AI's underlying computer program could be copyrighted, however; just not the results of its labors, because a human being wasn't instrumental in the creation of those results.)[51]

---

[51] *Id.*, at 906.8

WORKS FOR HIRE

"Works made for hire" are an important exception to the general rule for claiming copyright. To be clear, works made for hire *can* be copyrighted...just not by the person who created them!

When a work is made for hire, the author is not the individual who actually created the work; the party that *hired* the individual is considered the author and the copyright owner of the work. For instance, if you are employed by a magazine to write articles for the magazine, you are probably not the copyright holder of the articles.

There are two situations in which a work may be made for hire:

1. When the work is created by an employee as part of their regular work responsibilities, or
2. When a contractor and a hiring party enter into a specific written agreement that the work to be done by the contractor is to be considered a "work made for hire."

A work for hire happens when one party (the "employer") pays someone to create a work based on the employer's concept, and the employer has the right to direct and supervise the process of carrying out the work.[52]

On the other hand, if you are an independent contractor being paid to create something, then you most likely are the copyright holder, unless your contract states otherwise. The IRS defines an independent contract this way: "an individual is an independent contractor if the [person paying them] has the right to control or direct only the result of the work and not what will be done and how it will be done."[53] So as long as you control how you're doing the work, and the person paying only

---

[52] *Martha Graham School of Dance Foundation v. Martha Graham Center of Contemporary Dance*, 380 F.3d at 635 (2004)
[53] https://www.irs.gov/businesses/small-businesses-self-employed/independent-contractor-defined

has the right to specify the result, you're an independent contractor and hold copyright to the work.

There's a twist, though. (Of course there's a twist; this is law and there's always a twist.) Under some circumstances, an independent contractor may not be the copyright holder. That happens if the work is "specially ordered or commissioned for use;" and the parties sign a written contract that specifically states that the job is a work-for-hire; and the work falls into one of the following categories:[54]

- a contribution to a collective work,
- part of a motion picture or other audiovisual work,
- a translation,
- a supplementary work,
- a compilation,
- an instructional text,
- a test, and answer material for a test,
- an atlas.

The Copyright Office created a simple four-question test to determine whether or not a work is made for hire:[55]

1. Did the creator of the work create it while acting within the scope of their employment?
   Yes: The work is a work made for hire.
2. Is there a written agreement between the employer and the creator of the work?
   Yes: The work is a work made for hire.
3. Was the written agreement signed by both parties?
   Yes: The work is a work made for hire.
4. Did the written agreement clearly state that the work was a work made for hire?
   Yes: The work is a work made for hire.

---

[54] US Copyright Office, *Circular 9* (rev'd 2012)
[55] US Copyright Office *Circular 30* (rev'd 2021)

Basically, if your job requires you to create things, then the copyright to the things you create belongs to your employer. If you're freelancing, the copyright belongs to the person who pays you. The bottom line is that you're being paid by someone who is purchasing not just your work, but your whole bundle of sticks.

ⒸASE STUDY Between 1958 and 1963, renowned comic artist Jack Kirby produced 262 works for Marvel Comics, as a freelancer contracted by Stan Lee. He worked in his own studio, using his own tools, and at his own expense. Kirby's work was close and continuous, and Lee considered him one of Marvel's best artists. Most of Kirby's published work during that period was for Marvel, although he also did some work for other comics publishers. Working for Marvel, Kirby created such characters as The Incredible Hulk, Thor, Black Panther, Iron Man, the X-Men, and Doctor Doom. His work was performed for specific titles and under creative direction from Marvel, and Marvel had the right to reject his work or demand do-overs. His work was expected to conform with Marvel's house style specifications. As contractor, Jack Kirby assigned all copyrights in his work to Marvel.[56]

Jack Kirby died in 1994. In 2009, his surviving children attempted to "recapture" the assigned copyrights--recapture is possible in certain cases after 56 years (copyright assigned before 1978) or 35 years (copyright assigned after 1978). However, an estate's right to recapture copyright doesn't include assignments made under a work for hire agreement. Marvel (and its owner, Disney) sued the estate to block recapture.

The court ultimately found in favor of Marvel, concluding that the artwork was created under a work for hire relationship. "Kirby's completed pencil drawings, moreover, were generally not free-standing creative works, marketable to any publisher

---

[56] *Marvel v. Kirby*, 726 F.3d 119 (2013); see also Community for Creative Non-Violence v. Reid, 490 US 730 (1989).

as a finished or nearly finished product. They built on preexisting titles and themes that Marvel had expended resources to establish—and in which Marvel held rights—and they required both creative contributions and production work that Marvel supplied. That the works are now valuable is therefore in substantial part a function of Marvel's expenditures over and above the flat rate it paid Kirby for his drawings."

The decision was in the process of being appealed to the US Supreme Court, when the parties reached an out of court agreement. While the terms of that agreement are not public, the parties did issue this statement: "Marvel and the family of Jack Kirby have amicably resolved their legal disputes, and are looking forward to advancing their shared goal of honoring Mr. Kirby's significant role in Marvel's history."[57]

 So what do you take away from all this? Here are four key points to remember:

1. If a human didn't make it, it can't be copyrighted.
2. Copyright only protects things that are actually things: tangible stuff that can be shown to other people.
3. Things that don't have some element of creativity, uniqueness, or artistry can't be copyrighted.
4. If copyright isn't available, there may be other options like trademarks or patents.

---

[57] Rivera, J.," Why Kirby v. Marvel mattered." (Sept. 29, 2014) https://ew.com/article/2014/09/29why-kirby-v-marvel-mattered.

Chapter 3
Fair Use & Educational Use

YES, BUT... (AFFIRMATIVE DEFENSES)

So copyright infringement is copyright infringement, and it's bad. But sometimes, infringement is infringement, and it's OK.

Let's be clear: *there is no situation in which using someone else's copyrighted work without permission is not copyright infringement.* However, there are two major defenses to a claim of copyright infringement that, if successfully argued, will work to prevent a defendant from being punished for an acknowledged infringement.

Let's start with what an *affirmative defense* is. Its legal definition is something like "A defense in which the defendant introduces credible evidence, which will negate criminal liability or civil liability, even if it is proven that the defendant committed the alleged acts."[58]

What all that legal-ese means, in plain English, is that an affirmative defense is a way of saying, "Yes, but." The defendant

---

[58] Legal Information Institute, "Affirmative Defense" (https://www.law.cornell.edu/)

says, "*YES* I did the illegal act I'm accused of, *BUT* there's a legal principle that makes it OK that I did it."

Some examples of affirmative defenses in other areas of civil and criminal law are things like self-defense ("Yes I did it, but I was protecting myself"), entrapment ("Yes I did it, but only because they tricked me"), insanity ("Yes I did it, but I'm a total loon"), and *respondeat superior* (a fancy Latin phrase that basically means "Yes I did it, but blame my boss").

In copyright law, defendants can offer affirmative defenses such as minor use ("Yes I copied it, but it's just a couple of paragraphs"), or expired copyright ("Yes I did it, but it's been more than 70 years since the author's death").

But really, there are two big main affirmative defenses to copyright infringement: Fair Use and Educational Use.

In this chapter, we'll examine these two affirmative defenses. We'll also look at several interesting legal decisions that show how the principles of fair use are applied by courts.

The reason it's important for you to know about those affirmative defenses is not so much so that you can wiggle out of an infringement lawsuit (although that's certainly a plus). More importantly, you need to know about those defenses so you know when your content has been infringed—that is, someone violated your copyright in a way that makes it worthwhile to sue. It's also important to know them so that you have a good idea of what you can—and can't—do with other people's stuff.

CREDIT'S NOT ENOUGH

Some people mistakenly believe it's permissible to use a work (or portion of it) if an acknowledgment is provided. For example, they believe it's okay to use a photograph in a magazine as long as the name of the photographer is included, or long quotes as long as the source is cited.

This is not true.

Acknowledgment of the source material may be a consideration in a court's fair use determination, but it will not protect against a claim of infringement. When in doubt as to the right to use or acknowledge a source, seek the permission of the copyright owner.

FAIR USE

Copyright, as we know, is in the Constitution. Fair use, on the other hand, is statutory. But wherever it comes from, fair use is the law. Under statute, fair use is:

> ... use of a copyrighted work ... for purposes such as criticism, comment, news reporting, teaching (including multiple copies for classroom use), scholarship, or research.[59]

Courts look to four factors to determine whether or not a particular use is fair. Those factors are:

1. the *purpose and character* of the use, including whether the use is commercial or for nonprofit educational purposes;
2. the *nature* of the copyrighted work;
3. the *amount and substantiality* of the portion used compared to the copyrighted work as a whole; and
4. the effect of the use on the *potential market* for or value of the copyrighted work.[60]

Let's walk through those factors one at a time. Be warned, though: there may be four factors, but those factors often break down into multiple other elements, creating a kind of legal connect-the-dots, so it may not be quite as simple as it looks.

---

[59] 17 USC §107, Limitations on exclusive rights: Fair use
[60] *Id.*

Purpose and Character of the Use

The first factor is the purpose and character of the use. Courts will consider three different questions in order to determine the purpose and character. They are:

1. Is the use *commercial* or *nonprofit*?
2. Is there *limited access* to the work?
3. Is the use *transformative*?

Commercial or Nonprofit?

The first fair use factor refers mainly to how the copied material is being used. Copyright law favors the encouragement of scholarship, research, education, and commentary, so a judge is more likely to find that a use was fair if it's noncommercial, educational, scientific, or historical.

But Justice Sandra Day O'Connor famously wrote, "The Framers intended copyright itself to be the engine of free expression. By establishing a marketable right to the use of one's expression, copyright supplies the economic incentive to create and disseminate ideas."[61] That is, there's nothing inherently wrong with content being used for profit, and in fact copyright law is designed to encourage creators to make a little money from their efforts. But it's not designed for other people to profit from the copyright holder's work, and that's where the question of whether the infringed content was used for profit, or to support a commercial endeavor, comes into play.

However, even an educational or scientific use that is for commercial purposes may still be excused by the fair use doctrine. And just because a use is not for profit won't necessarily result in a finding of fair use; courts have made clear over and over again that the factors are weighed pretty much equally.

---

[61] *Harper and Row v. Nation Enterprises*, 471 US 539 (1985)

So this is as good a place as any to point out again that financial gain is NOT a necessary element of copyright infringement. It really doesn't matter if the infringer planned to get rich by selling copies of your work, or just planned to donate copies to a children's charity. Infringement is infringement.

However, America is a capitalist country, and our laws reflect that economic model, so depriving a copyright holder of potential financial gain is always going to be a serious element of copyright infringement. A commercial use will be looked at much more closely by a court than a non-commercial use, because US copyright law specifically protects the commercial interests of copyright holders.

Limited Access

The next element in defining the purpose and character of the use involves access. This consideration mostly focuses on the extent of exposure: How many people saw—or could have seen—the infringed work?

If the use involves private distribution (for instance, on a password-protected website or a one-time private gallery display) that factor will work in favor of a finding of fair use. On the other hand, if the use is widely published or distributed or broadcast, a court is likely to see more potential damage to the copyright holder.

Remember that the right to publish, perform, and distribute a work are all sticks in the copyright holder's bundle, and the law protects those sticks.

Transformative?

And finally, in looking at the purpose and character of the use, a court will ask if the use is transformative. Whether or not a use is transformative is defined by two questions:

1. Has the material taken from the original work been *transformed* by adding new expression or meaning?

2. Was *value added* to the original by creating new information, new aesthetics, new insights, and new understandings?

A use is transformative if it adds something new or different beyond simply repackaging or restating or reproducing the original. Although being transformative is not necessarily required for a court to find fair use, the goal of copyright law generally, as we know, is to "promote science and the arts." Transformative works—works that build on and expand and add to a copyrighted work—are doing exactly what the drafters of the Constitution wanted to have happen. The general view is that that Constitutional goal is achieved by the creation of transformative works.[62] That is, someone is moving science and the arts forward, based on the work of others who've come before them.

But keep in mind that these factors don't work independently of each other. "The more transformative the new work, the less important other things, like access or commercialism."[63]

CASE STUDY In 2003, artist and illustrator Derek Seltzer created "Scream Icon," a drawing of a screaming, contorted face.[64] Seltzer made copies of Scream Icon, some of which he glued on walls as street art in Los Angeles and elsewhere. Seltzer used the Scream Icon to identify himself and to advertise his gallery appearances.

In 2008, Roger Staub, a photographer and professional set-lighting and video designer, photographed a brick wall in Los Angeles that was covered in graffiti and posters—including a weathered and torn copy of "Scream Icon."

---

[62] *Campbell v. Acuff-Rose Music, Inc.*, 510 US 569, 584 (1994), citing *Sony Corp. of America v. Universal City Studios, Inc.*, 464 U. S. 417 (1984)
[63] *Campbell*
[64] *Seltzer v. Greenday, Inc., et al.*, No.11-56573, 725 F.3d 1170 (9th Cir. 2013)

"Scream Icon" by Derek Seltzer. From SELTZER v. GREEN DAY, INC., et al., No.11-56573, 725 F.3d 1170 (9th Cir. 2013), Appendices A and B

Staub was hired to create a four-minute video for use during Green Day concerts. His video depicts a brick alleyway covered in graffiti. Several days pass at a highly accelerated rate, during which graffiti artists come and go, adding new art, posters, and tags to the brick alleyway. Throughout the video, the center of the frame is dominated by an unchanging, but modified, Scream Icon. Staub used the photograph he had taken of the alley wall in Los Angeles, cut out the image of Scream Icon and modified it by adding a large red spray-painted cross over the middle of the screaming face. He also changed the contrast and color and added black streaks running down the right side of the image. The video, including "Scream Icon," was displayed during Green Day concerts, while the band played their song, "East Jesus Nowhere."

As soon as Seltzer became aware his poster was being used by Green Day, he sent the band a cease-and-desist letter, and Green Day promptly ceased and desisted, removing the video from their concerts.

Still seeking compensation for the use of his work, Seltzer sued Green Day for copyright infringement. Green Day's defense was that the use of the image was a fair use. The trial court found in favor of Green Day, and Seltzer appealed the decision.

The court of appeals applied the fair use analysis we just discussed, and concluded that Green Day's use of "Scream Icon" was transformative. The image was used as "raw materials" for a four-minute video, and was transformed from an interesting graphic of a screaming face referencing insider/outsider skateboard culture in LA to the centerpiece of a street-art video about religious angst. That's about as clear an example of transformation as you can get.

The artist didn't help his case by complaining that the use of "Scream Icon" "tainted the original message of the image and made it now synonymous with lyrics, a video, and concert tour that it was not originally intended to be used with." In other words, Greed Day *transformed* the graphic into something the artist hadn't intended.

With regard to commercial use, the court pointed out that while Green Day's concert was a commercial activity, the band's use of "Scream Icon" was only incidentally commercial; that is, Green Day never used it to market the concert, CDs, or merchandise, and it didn't appear on T-shirts sold at the venue.

The second factor is the nature of the work. The court found that because Seltzer had so widely published "Scream Icon," the court felt that Green Day's comparatively limited use wasn't so bad.

The third factor is how much of the original work was used—if the infringer used just a little bit, it's more likely to be fair use than if the infringer used the whole thing. The court acknowledged that Staub had copied pretty much 100% of "Scream Icon." But, said the court, it really wouldn't be possible for Staub to have used only 17% of Scream Icon to achieve what he was trying to create with his transformation: it was necessary to use it all. However, Staub also made major modifications to the image.

Finally, the fourth factor looks at the impact of the infringement on the potential market for the original work. Seltzer failed to demonstrate that the use of "Scream Icon" as a backdrop to a Green Day song performed in concert damaged the market for his prints of "Scream Icon." As Green Day's lawyers pointed out, the market for "Scream Icon" was in art shops and galleries, not rock concerts. They showed that they never sold the graphic, that it was used for only one four-minute song during a 3- hour show, and that it hadn't been used to promote the concert. The court found that there is no reasonable argument that Green Day had created a competing market for "Scream Icon."

In the end, the appeals court upheld the trial court's decision that Green Day's use of Seltzer's copyrighted work was an example of transformative use.

NATURE OF THE COPYRIGHTED WORK

The second element in the fair use analysis is the nature of the copyrighted work. Courts will consider a number of issues:

Fact or Imagination

Because the publication of facts and information benefits the public, factual works such as biographies or histories receive less protection from courts than fictional works such as plays or novels. An original poem or short story would receive stronger copyright protections from the courts than a factual article on the causes of diabetes.

Published or Unpublished

A published work will receive less protection from courts than an unpublished work. Courts presume an author has the right to control the first public appearance of their creative expression, and infringing an unpublished work deprives the author of that right.

Creative or Non-Creative

This factor focuses on the content that is being re-used. Courts are more protective of creative works (art, poetry, film) than non-creative works. If the original work is highly creative, like a song, movie, or TV show, courts will tend to apply very strong pro-creator protections. If the original work is less creative (like a phone directory, scientific data, or quotes from a historical record), courts may be more lenient toward a finding of fair use.

Out of Print or Orphan Works

A court will consider if the work is out of print, or if is an "orphan work," where the author or copyright holder is unknown or can't be found after a diligent search. In those cases, the use is more likely to be found to be fair.

AMOUNT AND SUBSTANTIALITY

The next element is the amount and substantiality of the copying. "Amount" refers to *how much* of the work is copied; "substantiality" refers to **how important** the copied part is to the value of the original work.

It's important to note that there is no specific measure of how much of a work may or may not be used. Even a small portion of a work may be its heart.

The court will weigh the following factors:

- length of original;
- the amount copied;
- whether the copied content is contiguous (a big chunk) or scattered (a lot of little pieces)

The less that is taken, the more likely that the copying will be excused as a fair use. However, even if a small portion of a work is taken, the copying will not be a fair use if the portion taken is the "heart" of the work.

In other words, a defendant is more likely to run into problems if they take the most memorable or important part of a work.

MARKET EFFECT

Finally, the court will consider effect that the infringement has on the market for the work.

While financial gain is not a requirement, depriving a creator of the right to financially benefit from their creation is a serious consideration for courts. In fact, on more than one occasion the Supreme Court has referred to market effect as the most important of the four factors in making a determination of fair use.[65]

If a plaintiff can demonstrate that the infringing use could adversely affect the potential market for the copyrighted work—not only causing harm to the market for the original work, but also harm to the market for existing and potential derivative works and secondary markets, which might include translations, movie rights, or images on phone cases or coffee mugs.

So the basic question for the court is, does the infringing use deprive the copyright owner of income or undermine a new or potential market for the copyrighted work?

The bottom line is, well, the bottom line: Depriving a copyright owner of income is very likely to trigger an infringement suit.

Utilitarianism is the dominant purpose of American copyright law: encouraging the creation of new stuff and the generating of new ideas, and making sure that creators are compensated *and* that the ideas are available to the public, where they'll presumably generate more new ideas and...more ideas. Put

---

[65] See, for example, *Warner Bros. Entertainment, Inc. v. RDR Books*, 575 F.Supp.2d 513 (S.D. N.Y. 2008) (Harry Potter books); *Rogers v. Koons*, 960 F.2d 301 (2d Cir. 1992) (photograph reproduced as sculpture); *Campbell v. Acuff-Rose Music*, 510 US 569 (1994) (song parody).

another way, according to utilitarian theory, copyright law provides the incentive of exclusive rights for a limited time to creators as a way of motivating them to create culturally valuable works. Without this incentive, creators might not invest the time, energy, and money necessary to create their works because of the risk that the works might be copied cheaply and easily by free-riders, and eliminate creators' ability to profit from their works.

PARODY

Another form of fair use is parody. Parody is a form of satire that imitates the characteristic style of a particular writer, musician, artist, speaker or genre using deliberate exaggeration for a comic effect in order to express an opinion or observation about the subject content.

Parody and satire aren't the same thing, even though they're often used interchangeably. Satire is the use of humor, ridicule, irony or exaggeration to make fun of or criticize a person or institution. Parody uses an original work to express an opinion *about that work*, while satire may use an original work to make fun of something else. Parody is considered a fair use; satire is not.

A parodist is permitted to borrow quite a bit, even the "heart" of the original work: "the heart is also what most readily conjures up the [original] for parody, and it is the heart at which parody takes aim."[66]

Market Effect

Parody is given a slightly different fair use analysis with regard to the impact on the market.

Courts acknowledge that a parody may diminish or even destroy the market value of the original work; the parody may

---

[66] *Campbell v. Acuff-Rose Music*, 510 US 569 (1994)

be so good that the public can never take the original work seriously again. And courts are OK with that.

"The economic effect of a parody ... is not its potential to destroy or diminish the market for the original—any bad review can have that effect—but whether it fulfills the demand for the original."[67]

Some examples might help. Weird Al Yankovic's songs, for instance, are parody: they mimic the style of the original, and make fun of both the original song and some other social issue. So a song like "Tacky" is a parody of Pharrell Williams' "Happy"; "Perform This Way" is a parody of Lady Gaga's "Born This Way," "Amish Paradise" is a parody of Coolio's "Gansta's Paradise"; "All About the Pentiums" is a parody of Puff Daddy's "All About the Benjamins"; and "Eat It" is a parody of Michael Jackson's "Beat It."[68]

The 2012-2019 TV comedy "Veep" is a satire of politics and politicians; it doesn't directly refer to a specific person or thing. "Bridgerton," on the other hand, while not specifically referring to any individual work, could be construed as a parody of 19th century romantic novels, and period romance movies and shows generally. It consciously uses the tropes, cliches, characters, and conflicts of Victorian romance to highlight their absurdity, sexism, and classism.

If you're creating a parody, you're using the protected work to make a larger comment about something. You'll recall from earlier that parody is *a form of satire that imitates the characteristic style of a particular writer, musician, artist, speaker or genre using deliberate exaggeration for a comic effect in order to express an opinion or observation about the subject content.* Parody requires that you're not just making a joke or a visual pun; you need to have something to say. Satire is the use

---

[67] Fisher v. Dees, 794 F.2d 432 (9th Cir. 1986)
[68] You can check out those song parodies and others at http://weirdal.com/videos/

of humor, ridicule, irony or exaggeration to make fun of or expose and criticize a person or institution. Parody is considered a fair use; satire is not.

Someone could do a parody of a Taylor Swift song, and that would work because people would likely know the song and so they'd "get" why the parody was funny. Someone could do a parody of a song I made up in the shower this morning, but that would be pretty pointless because no one knows that song.

Parody can be challenging to recognize, though. For parody to be successful, it has to be identifiable with the original work that it's parodying. For example, Saturday Night Live does a parody of the TV show "Empire," but it doesn't look anything like "Empire:" the actors play characters who don't appear in "Empire," the plot elements have nothing to do with "Empire," and the sketch is about a French restaurant instead of a Black-owned recording label. That's not going to succeed as parody. *Some direct copying of the original is vital to the nature of parody.*

But it's easier to say that than to make a rule about it, so parody has to be looked at by a court using the relevant fair use factors. Essentially, the only way to determine whether or not a use is parody—and therefore presumptively a fair use—is for a court to look at the unique facts of that particular case and apply the fair use factors:

"The fact that parody can claim legitimacy for some appropriation does not, of course, tell either parodist or judge much about where to draw the line. ... [P]arody may or may not be fair use, and [the] suggestion that any parodic use is presumptively fair has no ... justification in law or fact. ... Accordingly, parody, like any other use, has to work its way through the relevant factors, and be judged case by case, in light of the ends of the copyright law."[69]

---

[69] *Campbell v. Acuff-Rose Music, Inc.*, 510 US 569 (1994)

CASE STUDY

J. K. Rowling wrote the Harry Potter series, creating a vast and complex magical landscape populated with a wide variety of distinct characters. Rowling published the first Harry Potter book in 1997 and over the next 10 years, she published another 6 titles in the series, as well as two companion books (a history of Quidditch and a bestiary. More than 500 million copies of the books have been sold in 80 languages, amounting to total sales of the books alone of nearly $25 million, plus another $8 billion in revenue from film adaptations. In interviews, Rowling has said that she might create an encyclopedia to define and explain that world, but has never done so.[70]

The Potter books spawned innumerable fan sites sprinkled across the Internet, featuring art, derivative stories featuring the characters (which Rowling does not discourage) and opinion, chat, and criticism. One of the most successful of these sites, established in 2000, is The Harry Potter Lexicon, created and maintained by Potter super-fan Steven Vander Ark. It's designed to be a database for readers, describing all the elements of the books in great detail. The website featured Vander Ark's descriptive lists of spells, characters, creatures, and magical items from Harry Potter with hyperlinks to cross-referenced entries. Vander Ark developed an A-to-Z index to each list to allow users to search for entries alphabetically.

In August 2007, Van der Ark was approached by the publisher of RDR books about publishing the Lexicon website content in book form. At his first meeting with the publisher, Van der Ark asked specifically whether or not publishing the site might raise a copyright issue. The publisher assured him that they had determined that publishing the Lexicon website content in book form was a perfectly legal fair use. So Vander Ark proceeded to transcribe the website content into a book format. The manuscript was over 400 pages long and contained 2,437

---

[70] *Warner Bros. Entertainment Inc. et al v. RDR Books et al*, No. 1:2007cv09667 - Document 92 (S.D.N.Y. 2008)

alphabetical entries covering every creature, spell, potion, character, object, event, and place in the Harry Potter novels. It also included an acknowledgment that it was based on the work of J.K. Rowling, who it says holds the copyright on the Harry Potter universe.

Warner Bros and Rowling immediately sued, seeking a temporary injunction to prevent publication on the basis that publication of the Lexicon would infringe on Rowling's copyright and that she has openly and repeatedly expressed her interest in publishing an encyclopedia covering all seven books. Warner Bros pointed out that "There is a big difference between a free fan website and a for-profit book that attempts to make money out of Ms. Rowling's original works."

In its decision, the court conducted a painstakingly detailed comparison of the Potter books and the Lexicon, finding numerous instances of text from the novels being freely incorporated into the encyclopedia entries without attribution. The court then walked through all the elements of fair use, concluding that the Lexicon book was an infringement of Rowling's copyright.

While the Lexicon was transformative, wrote the court, RDR failed to establish a case for fair use. Rowling and Warner Bros had based part of their claim on the Lexicon being a derivative work, which you'll recall is one of the sticks in the copyright bundle.

The court granted a permanent injunction against publishing the Lexicon book, and applied statutory damages of $6,750 (more than the Lexicon site had earned from advertising during its entire existence).

(The Lexicon site is still online, unbothered by Rowling, at https://www.hp-lexicon.org/)

EDUCATIONAL USE

We've all heard it from teachers and students and trainers and speakers: "This is copyrighted, but it's OK for me to use it because I'm doing it for educational purposes." But just because we've heard it doesn't mean it's as simple as all that, or that it's even true. Because it's not. There are, in fact, very clear and specific limits on what can be considered a valid educational use.

Educational use is a law.[71] As long as your use complies with the requirements of the law, your copyright infringement is, by definition, not infringement. However, simply saying "it's for educational use" just isn't enough.

> *Just because you stand in front of a classroom and talk doesn't mean you are free to steal other peoples' property.*

The "Classroom Use Guidelines" established in 17 USC § 107 and discussed at length in the accompanying House Report, establish the basic rules governing the educational use defense.

The rules are pretty specific and clear, which is why there's not a lot of important case law in this area. Mostly, courts just apply the general rules, and tend to find more often than not that the educational use defense doesn't apply.

Of course, while educational use may be relevant to students and professors, it's generally not something that comes up a lot for creative folks, unless your property is what's being used.

But anyway, we hear it a lot so let's see if I can ruin the fun for you.

We know that there's an "educational use" exception because it's in federal law:

---

[71] 17 USC § 107

> [T]he fair use of a copyrighted work, including such use by reproduction in copies ... for purposes such as criticism, comment, news reporting, teaching (including multiple copies for classroom use), scholarship or research, **is not an infringement of copyright.**[72]

That's pretty clear, but it doesn't really give much detail. To know how to apply this statute, courts look to the legislative history—what Congress said about what a law is supposed to do while they were drafting and debating it. Looking at that history is how courts determine what the law is supposed to prevent or encourage, and how Congress thought it should be applied. For the most part, courts defer to legislative intent, because the people who made the law are probably (though not always) in the best position to know what it means and what they meant it to do.

Here, House Report 1476 "Classroom Use Guidelines" is often cited by courts as they determine whether or not educational use applies.[73]

Those guidelines are pretty simple:

Multiple copies are permitted for classroom use by instructors, provided that the copying meets the following six requirements:

> (1) the copying meets the test of **brevity**
>
> (2) the copying meets the test of **spontaneity**
>
> (3) only a **limited number** of copies are made from the works of any one author or from any one collective work
>
> (4) each copy contains a **notice of copyright**
>
> (5) the copying **does not substitute** for the purchase of "books, publishers' reprints or periodicals" and

---

[72] 17 USC § 107
[73] See, e.g., https://www.copyright.gov/history/law/clrev_94-1476.pdf

(6) the student is not charged any more than **the actual cost** of copying

Let's take a look at each of those requirements individually.

Brevity

Brevity is the first requirement, and it means just what it suggests: Educators are not permitted to copy all of Chapter Twelve of *Harry Potter and the Bundle of Sticks* to distribute to their class.

Fortunately, this is unlike the very vague standard for fair use in copyright (you'll remember that a short passage or a whole chapter can be equally damaging, and it's up to the court to decide how much is too much). For the specific educational use defense, Congress has provided very specific guidelines.[74]

- Poetry: less than 250 words or not more than two pages. (This makes sense because most poems are pretty short, except for the long ones.)
- Prose (fiction or nonfiction): less than 2,500 words, or 10% of the work, whichever is *less*. So if it's a very short book with only 3000 words, only 300 words could be copied. But *War and Peace* is a very long novel, and has 587,287 words, so 10% would be nearly 59,000 words. That's too many: only 2,500 can be copied. And that's your math for today.
- Copies of Illustrations are limited to one chart, graph, diagram, drawing, cartoon, photograph, or picture per book or periodical issue or website.
- "Special" works—that is, anything that doesn't fit into the first three categories—or works of less than 2,500 words: educators can copy an excerpt comprising not

---

[74] 17 USC § 107, Limitations on exclusive rights: Fair use; H.R. 2223 §107 Agreement on Guidelines for Classroom Copying in Not-For-Profit Educational Institutions

more than two pages and containing not more than 10% of the words and illustrations.

That final "special" category would also refer to movies and music, which is why, in amateur "reaction videos" on YouTube, where YouTubers record themselves listening to new songs or watching new music videos, you often see them wearing headphones, or jump-cutting from the start to the finish of a song. They are being compliant with the educational use requirements, which also apply to works of criticism.

Spontaneity

The second requirement basically means an instructor wakes up in the morning two hours before class and is utterly inspired by an editorial cartoon in the morning paper that's absolutely relevant to morning's day's class. The instructor is allowed to photocopy it for distribution in that class, because there's not enough time to contact the paper to ask for permission.

Even so, they have to give credit.

(I'd show an example here, but for obvious reasons I can't really do that.)

OTHER GUIDELINES

Brevity and spontaneity are the biggest considerations in deciding if a use is educational or not. But there are a few more.[75]

- You can't create your own collection of your favorite 2,500 words from your fifteen favorite books and publish it.
- You can't photocopy the key pages from a textbook and then tell your students not to buy the book.

---

[75] H.R. 2223 §107 Agreement on Guidelines for Classroom Copying in Not-For-Profit Educational Institutions

- Anytime copyrighted works are used, the copyright notice must be clearly displayed.
- The copying can't be "directed by a higher authority." That doesn't have anything to do with Zeus appearing to you in a dream and telling you to copy and distribute 2,500 words from *The Hunger Games*. It means that your boss can't tell you to do the spontaneous, brief copying. It means that a university dean or department chair can't be "inspired" some morning by an editorial cartoon and require all professors to include it in class.
- "Educational use" can only be invoked once. Educators aren't allowed to be spontaneously moved by the same editorial cartoon in their Monday class, and then their Tuesday class, and then all their Spring classes, and then again in Summer, and then again in Fall. After that first use, they have plenty of time to get permission from the copyright holder.
- Instructors can't copy "consumable works." That doesn't mean they can't copy delicious pies, it means they can't make a copy of a workbook or a coloring book or a day planner—those works are created and published specifically to be bought and used once: to be written in, or colored in; copying them defeats their commercial purpose. And we know defeating a copyright holder's commercial purpose is frowned upon.
- Finally, students can't be charged more than the actual cost of reproducing the content. That is, a professor can't create printed course packs that cost $15 to copy at the copy shop, charge students $30, and then pocket the proceeds to buy a nice dinner later.

 **So what do you take away from all this? Four simple points to remember:**

1. All the sticks in the bundle of rights belong to the copyright holder, whether he or she chooses to do anything with them or not.
2. Parody is a protected fair use; satire is not.
3. To determine if someone's use of a copyrighted work is fair or not, courts look to four factors:
   - the purpose and character of the use;
   - the nature of the copyrighted work;
   - the amount and substantiality of the portion used; and
   - the effect of the use on the potential value of the copyrighted work.
4. Educational use isn't a blanket permission to use other people's stuff; there are specific requirements and expectations.

PART 2

COPYRIGHT & YOUR CREATIVE WORK

THE FIX IS IN

The United States Copyright Office offers examples of specific items of visual arts that are protected by copyright[76]. In the following chapters, we'll take a look at some of these categories of creative expression and show how copyright law applies to them.

A visual art work must be a new or derivative work that's "fixed" in a "tangible medium of expression" in order to be protected by copyright.[77] "Fixed" means, basically, that the work has to be in a form that allows it to be "perceived, reproduced, or otherwise communicated for a period of more than a transitory duration."[78]

The Copyright Office provides a non-exhaustive list of types of materials or media that qualify as "tangible," including canvas,

---

[76] US Copyright, Circular 40: *Copyright Registration for Pictorial, Graphic, and Sculptural Works* (rev. 2015)
[77] 17 USC § 102(a)
[78] 17 USC § 101

paper, clay, stone, metal, collages, prints, photographs, digital files, holograms, diagrams, patterns, models, and architecture.[79]

The Copyright Office won't register a work that's created in a medium that's not intended to exist permanently, or in a medium that's constantly changing.[80] So, for example, an ice sculpture or sandcastle couldn't be copyrighted, nor (as we see in the "Gardening") can an art installation made of wildflowers and prairie grasses.

Unfortunately, there's no sneaky way around that requirement. Taking a photo of a non-fixed work (that wildflower installation, say, or a fireworks display) doesn't make the underlying work fixed; while the photograph *is* fixed and *could* be copyrighted, the subject of the photo is not and couldn't be. Similarly, a written description of the idea for a work of visual art that's in an unfixed medium may be copyrighted as prose (though not as an idea), but it still doesn't copyright the unfixed work.[81]

THE THINGS YOU DO…

In the following chapters, we'll look at a wide range of creative activities, arranged within twelve broad categories. The general copyright concepts we've covered apply to these activities, of course, but here we'll consider the unique copyright issues that are specifically relevant to each type of creative work.

---

[79] US Copyright Office, *Compendium*, Chapter 900: Visual Art Works, § 903.1, 904 (rev'd 2021)
[80] *Id.*, § 904
[81] *Id.*

Chapter 4

Crafts

JEWELRY

Jewelry designs are typically protected under the US copyright law as sculptural works.[82] Jewelry designs are considered "works of artistic craftsmanship," which are protected "insofar as their form but not their mechanical or utilitarian aspects are concerned."[83]

Jewelry includes any decorative article that is intended to be worn as a personal adornment, regardless of whether it is hung, pinned, or clipped onto the body (such as necklaces, bangles, or earrings) or pinned, clipped, or sewn onto clothing (such as brooches, pins, or beaded motifs).[84]

Separability

The separability rule applies to jewelry as well, because many items of jewelry do double duty as useful articles of clothing (like belts, for instance, or hair clips, or any jeweled or beaded design applied to garments and accessories. However, when

---

[82] US Copyright Office, *Compendium*, Chapter 900: Jewelry, § 908 (rev'd 2021)
[83] 17 USC § 101; 37 CFR § 202.8(a)
[84] US Copyright Office, *Compendium*, Chapter 900: Jewelry, § 908 (rev'd 2021)

these types of works are fixed onto clothing and/or accessories, they may be registered only if they are separable from the clothing and/or accessories.

> *The Copyright Office's grant of copyright in a piece of jewelry will not include the "mechanical or utilitarian aspects of the jewelry" such as clasps, chains, prongs, etc.*[85]

To determine if an item of jewelry that's part of a useful article can be copyrighted, the Copyright Office goes through a three-step process:

1. Examine the item as a whole for features that "can be perceived as a two or three-dimensional work of art separate from the useful article."[86]
2. If the answer to the first question is Yes, then the Office will determine if that feature could be separated from the useful article.[87]
3. If it can be separated, the Copyright Office will finally determine whether or not it demonstrates enough creativity to qualify for copyright protection.[88]

©ase Study — A metalworker built a successful business designing, manufacturing, and selling beautiful, elaborate, art nouveau belt buckles, in silver and gold. A competitor copies and sells the buckles in cheaper metals, claiming that there's no copyright violation because of the "useful article" exclusion.[89] Now, a belt is certainly a useful article, with the admirable function of keeping your pants from falling down around your knees at inappropriate times, and a belt buckle is pretty vital to that function. In this case, though, the court held that the unique

---

[85] *Id.*
[86] *Star Athletica, LLC, v. Varsity Brands, Inc.*, 137 S.Ct. 1002 (2017)
[87] *Id.*
[88] *Id.*
[89] *Kieselstein-Cord v. Accessories by Pearl, Inc* - 632 F.2d 989 (1980)

buckle design was distinct from the functional components of the belt, and so was protected by copyright.

> *The US Copyright Office may register jewelry designs if they are sufficiently creative or expressive. The Office will not register pieces that do not satisfy this requirement, such as commonplace design elements arranged in a common or obvious manner. Common de minimis designs include solitaire rings, simple diamond stud earrings, plain bangle bracelets, simple hoop earrings, among other commonly used designs, settings, and gemstone cuts.*[90]

POTTERY

Ceramic and clay works pretty clearly fall under the copyright law's provisions for visual arts and sculptural works ("carvings, ceramics, figurines, maquettes, molds, relief sculptures")[91] unless they're mostly functional, like creamers or drinkware, in which case it might be tougher to make a convincing case. Remember, copyright law doesn't like utilitarian objects.

But things that *could* be functional but could *also* be stand-alone art objects suitable for display—pots, vases, bowls, even plates—stand a better chance of being copyrighted if they have some unique decorative components: a milk pitcher in the shape of a cow, for instance, or a vase in the shape of a human head.

Again, though, remember that copyright can extend only to the unique elements of a pottery, not the pottery itself.[92] Your

---

[90] US Copyright Office, *Compendium*, Chapter 900: Jewelry, § 908.2 (rev'd 2021)

[91] US Copyright Office, Circular 40: "Copyright Registration for Works of the Visual Arts" (rev'd 2015)

[92] This is an area in which a design patent would protect the whole look of, say, a clay pot. But design patents can be expensive and time-consuming to acquire. Unless you're doing industrial-level commercial production or charging very high prices, the patent path is probably not worthwhile.

protection also applies only to the specific pottery work; nothing stops anyone from making a pitcher that resembles your cow, as long as it's not a direct copy and has clearly distinguishing features. (See the Case Study under Needlework, Fabrics & Quilts for an example of how courts test for distinguishing features.)

The more your pottery works are sculptural rather than functional the easier it will be to copyright them.

Obviously, making a mold from an existing work violates that work's copyright, so don't do that. Making little ceramic statuettes of Mickey Mouse may seem like a cute idea, but the Disney corporation will take a very dim view—and while Disneyland may be the happiest place on earth, a meeting with Disney's legal team regarding an infringement is probably the saddest place on earth.

STAINED-GLASS

Stained-glass works are generally copyrightable as "pictorial, graphic, and sculptural works" under copyright law. The same limitations apply to stained glass works, of course, as to other creative work.

If you're reproducing stained-glass works you've found in, for instance, an old church, it's likely that any copyright that may have once been held by the original artist has long since expired. However, the windows are still a part of the church architecture, so you would need to obtain permission from the church to reproduce the windows.

Some things to keep in mind:

Like any other creative work, if you produce an original work of stained-glass art, you hold the copyright. However, be careful when producing stained-glass "versions" of other works.

For instance, if you wanted to make an exact stained-glass version of Mondrian's *Composition with Yellow, Red, Black, Blue, and Gray,* you'd want to know if the original image was still under copyright.

Piet Mondrian (1872-1944), Composition with Yellow, Red, Black, Blue, and Gray (A 9864) Amsterdam - Stedelijk Museum – 1920. Photo by TxllxT TxllxT, Creative Commons Attribution-Share Alike 4.0

Piet Mondrian died in 1944, but *Composition* was created in 1920—before 1978—so the rule that applies is public domain 95 years after creation, or 2015[93]. You'd be OK doing your stained-glass replica, but it's better to be safe than sued. [94]

---

[93] US Copyright Office, Circular 38B: Copyright Restoration Under the URAA (rev. 2013)

[94] This example is a little tricky, due to international treaties. The US passed the Uruguay Round Agreements Act (URAA) in 1994—one of many international treaties, such as the Berne Convention, that influence US copyright law. The purpose of the URAA was basically to protect works by non-US creators that had become public domain under US law but not under the law of the author's country. Since Mondrian was Dutch and Composition was created in the Netherlands, European copyright applies. Under EU law, copyright expires 70 years after the author's death, just like in the US, or in this case 2014. So either way you're good. But be careful.

TOYS

The Copyright Office recognizes some toys are copyrightable "sculptural works."[95] It all boils down, though, to whether or not a court concludes that your toy is useful.[96]

In one toy-centered case[97], the court held that toys do not have an intrinsic function other than the portrayal of the real item. They are therefore not useful items and are protectable by copyright. Another court found that doll clothing *is* protectable (even though full-size clothing is useful), because dolls don't feel cold or worry about modesty.[98]

The statutory definition of "useful article" suggests that toys can be copyrighted. To be a "useful article," the item must have "an intrinsic utilitarian function that is not merely to portray the appearance of the article." As a rule, toys are not considered useful articles for purposes of registration, because in most cases they merely portray their own appearance or the item that the work represents.[99] That is, a toy airplane is merely a model that portrays a real airplane. Other than the portrayal of a real airplane, a toy airplane has no intrinsic utilitarian function.

The same might not be said, though, for toys that *do* have a useful function, like toy tools or toys designed to teach language, or math, or scientific principles.

Here's a catch for toymakers, though: if your toy is based on a protected property (copyrighted and/or trademarked) you will

---

[95] US Copyright Office, *Compendium*: Visual Art Works Chapter 900, §903.1 (rev. 2021)
[96] Rachel Pearlman, "IP Frontiers: From planes to dolls: Copyright challenges in the toy industry," Daily Register, September 17, 2012 (https://nydailyrecord.com/2012/09/17/ip-frontiers-from-planes-to-dolls-copyright-challenges-in-the-toy-industry/)
[97] *Gay Toys Inc. v. Buddy L. Corp.*, 703 F.2d 970, 973 (6th Cir. 1983)
[98] *Mattel, Inc. v. MGA Entertainment, Inc.*, 616 F.3d 904, 916 (9th Cir. 2010)
[99] 17 USC § 101

need the owner's permission to produce and sell or distribute your toy.[100] Similarly, if your doll is based on an actual living person, you'll need their permission. (Remember that "living person" includes people who have been dead for less than 70 years, as well as animals who are sufficiently well-known to have their identity rights protected.)[101] If your toy is based on a branded and trademarked property (for instance, a toy version of a Toyota Prius), you will need permission from the manufacturer of the original property, and if your toy is based on established, protected characters from books, movies, or television, again, you'll need a license.

The good news, though, is that toys based on government-owned properties (NASA's Mars rovers, military vehicles, rockets, etc.) fall into the same category as government publications; you probably don't need permission to create toy versions—although be careful, because copyright, trademark, or design patents on some of those properties may still be held by the company that designed and built them. You'll need to do some research, or else just make up your own designs.

WOODWORK

Remember that *copyright does not protect useful items*. So if you're making a bookcase or bench, you can hold copyright on any *original* decorative elements, but not the entire object. Note that copyright will only extend to original decorative elements; things like simple grooves, medallions, and standard floral

---

[100] As has been pointed out before, it's irrelevant whether or not you profit from your infringing activity: if someone steals your car, you really don't care if the thief uses it to deliver meals to the elderly or sells it on the black market—you just want your car back.

[101] The laws surrounding an individual's physical appearance and identity rights are many and complex, and go well beyond the scope of this book. If you're designing a toy or other artwork that depicts an actual individual, you should definitely consult an IP attorney.

elements may not be protected, but unique marquetry, inlays, and custom carving can be.

If you're building furniture, you can't copyright the finished product—it's a useful item. What you *can* copyright, though, are any drawings or plans you've created that are, essentially, creative artworks on their own. Similarly, when you use someone else's plans for a project, their copyright is on the actual printed drawings, not the completed useful object.

As discussed earlier, if the useful item you're creating in your woodshop doesn't look like a useful item (a coatrack that looks like hands, for example, or a liquor cabinet shaped like a bear) it's more likely that it can be copyrighted as an artistic object.

That said, the situation here is similar to that of our previous discussion of fabric patterns: whoever published the plans you're using may have limited the uses to which finished products can be put. There may be a maximum number of units allowed, or a no-commercial-use clause. It's up to you to figure that out.

 So what do you take away from all this? Four simple points to remember:

1. Copyright does not protect "useful items," so be as creative as you can.
2. "Separability" means that the utilitarian aspects of a work can be distinguished from artistic, copyrightable elements.
3. Unlike clothing for humans, clothing for dolls is copyrightable because it serves no useful function (except for the doll of course).
4. Toys and pottery can both be considered sculptural works.

Chapter 5
Graphic Arts

"Graphic Arts" covers a lot of territory: basically any two-dimensional representations, decorations, writing or printing on flat surfaces.[102] So typically this includes drawings, sketches, cartoons, calligraphy, and graphic design. That said, we're expanding the definition a little here, to include less traditional graphic arts likes tattoos and graffiti, despite their unconventional media.

CARTOONS, COMIC STRIPS, & COMIC BOOKS

Cartoons, comic strips, and comic books usually include both artistic and literary components, but copyright can be registered in only one. A comic artist who also writes the stories and text needs to decide whether to register the work as artistic or literary.

It's important to know that you can't copyright a series of comics or the superhero who appears in most of the issues (but see **Characters**). You can only copyright an individual work. So if you've created a 20-issue set of comics, you'll need to apply for

---

[102] "Graphic arts," *Merriam-Webster.com Dictionary*, https://www.merriam-webster.com/dictionary/graphicarts.

individual copyrights for all twenty (unless you've cleverly stitched them together into a single volume).

> *Comic works cannot be aggregated simply for the purpose of registration; instead they must have been first distributed to the public in the packaged unit.*

Comics are frequently the result of collaboration among multiple contributors—one or more artists, a writer, a letterer, a colorist, even a cover designer. Each contributor may be able to claim copyright over a particular aspect of the work. For instance, the publisher may own the characters or story arc. If the other contributors are hired by the publisher as employees or freelancers or under work for hire agreements, then copyright is held by the publisher alone. But if a group of artists work together on a comic, the group can apply for joint copyright as a multiauthor work—a process that's a little more complicated and time-consuming, but doable. Alternatively, one member of the group can hold copyright with everyone's agreement.

CHARACTERS

Let's say you've created an original cartoon character. You can copyright the original, visual aspects of the character, since (as far as I know) it's a unique character. You can protect how the character looks—its physical attributes, like facial features, body shape, clothing, facial features. Your copyright will only protect the visual characteristics reflected in the copies you send to the Copyright Office, but not the character's "unfixed" characteristics, like its personality, its funny way of talking, its backstory, or the general idea behind it. Your copyright will also not include the character's name, because as a general rule names are not copyrightable.[103] As is often the case, though, you

---

[103] *Id.*, § 911

can look to trademark law for guidance on protecting character names.

Copyright of characters is not dependent on the medium, so it doesn't matter if your character will appear in print, online, or in movies.

If your character strongly resembles an existing copyrighted character, or is a derivative work based on such an existing character, you should be sure to have permission and a license from the copyright holder before running off with one of the sticks in their bundle.

FAN ART

You'll find it all over Artist's Alleys at pop culture conventions, in booths at flea markets and fairs, and all across the Internet: beautiful, usually respectful, almost always creative and sometimes artistically amazing interpretations of superheroes, characters from television and movies, and other pop culture icons.

OK, so here's the bad news: Fan art is, per se, a copyright violation. It doesn't matter if it's respectful of the original, or acknowledges the copyright holder. It doesn't matter that it's done out of love for a franchise, or that it adds exciting new dimensions to an established (and legally protected) character. Fan art, at its core, is a derivative work of someone else's copyrighted content that's not transformative enough to be a fair use—the whole point of fan art is that it's recognizable as a character in an established franchise. If it was transformative enough to be fair use, it wouldn't be "good" fan art any more. As an added bonus, a lot of popular characters are trademarked, too, so it's a double-whammy of exposure to infringement lawsuits.

That is, if your Spider-Man is recognizably Marvel's Spider-Man (which he probably is, since the nature of fan art is to recognizably depict the thing that the artist is a fan of), it's infringement even though Peter Parker is drawn in your unique artistic style. As we saw in our fair use discussion, if your art is somehow parodying Spider-Man, or commenting on the commercial nature of modern entertainment, you *might* be able to claim it's fair use as a parody. But more likely, it's just copyright infringement.

Interestingly, many major authors, publishers, and studios seem to tolerate fan art, since there's so much of it at cons and so few big infringement lawsuits against individuals. That doesn't make it OK, of course; it's still 100% illegal, even if the copyright holders look the other way. It's an interesting situation, because sometimes copyright holders will look the other way, and sometimes they will land on fan-artists like a giant Acme anvil in a Road Runner cartoon.

For the most part, DC and Marvel tolerate quite a bit of fan-art, but Disney is uncompromising in its defense of its *Star Wars* and Mickey-related properties. Paramount, on the other hand, has shown a tolerance for fan-art related to its *Star Trek* franchise—unless fans take it too far.

One easy way to avoid problems is to stick to public domain characters. While you can't legitimately produce non-infringing artwork based on Disney's character Ariel from the film, *The Little Mermaid*, nothing stops you from producing artwork based on the nameless mermaid from Hans Christian Andersen's story, "The Little Mermaid." Just be crystal clear about which mermaid you're depicting, and don't give your Hans Christian Andersen mermaid bright red hair and a best friend who's a snail who sings with a Trinidad accent.

Another solution is to avoid basing your work on existing characters altogether.

But if you insist, there are some things you can do. Note, though, that unless you're producing a parody or other fair use (which you probably aren't), these won't save you from a cease-and-desist letter or lawsuit.

1. Do your research: if an author or studio has made a clear statement about fan art, find out and respect it.

2. Be non-commercial: studios and authors tend to be much more tolerant of "labors of love" than they are of other people making money from their properties.

3. And finally, if you're asked by the copyright holder to stop producing fan art...stop.

Fan Artist Partner Programs

Some commercial outlets for artists have entered into blanket licensing agreements with copyright holders, so that their participating artists can legally sell *Star Trek*-inspired t-shirts and other products.

Redbubble and TeePublic, for instance, have negotiated with a wide variety of copyright owners who have agreed to participate in partner programs. Fan artists can submit their designs and receive approval to market them on the sites. Redbubble's program is described here: https://www.redbubble.com/partner-program#guidelines, and TeePublic's is here: https://teepublic.zendesk.com/hc/en-us/sections/360004233273-Fan-Art-Program

CALLIGRAPHY

Unfortunately, typefaces, fonts, lettering, calligraphy, and typographic ornamentation are not copyrightable.[104] That's because letters and words are considered the "building blocks" of expression, and calligraphy or unique fonts are simply variations on those building blocks.

> "The [Copyright] Office typically refuses claims based on individual alphabetic or numbering characters, sets or fonts of related characters, fanciful lettering and calligraphy, or other forms of typeface. This is true

---

[104] 37 CFR § 202.1(a), (e).

regardless of how novel and creative the shape and form of the typeface characters may be."[105]

As is often the case in law, however, the Copyright Office does recognize some limited exceptions to this general rule of non-copyrightability:

- Original graphic art that uses non-letter objects to suggest letters (a horse for a lower-case "h" for instance, or a snake that looks like a capital "S").[106]

Typographical flourishes, like swirls, curlicues, and similar decorations added to the beginning or end of letters, may be copyrightable *if* you can demonstrate that they're unique artistic creations tacked-on to utilitarian letters.[107]

Graphic designers can often rely on trademark law to protect their work more than copyright, which offers fewer protections due to functionality concerns. That's why you often see corporate logos, brand names, movie titles, and similar designs carrying a TM symbol.

BOARD GAMES

So you have a great idea for a board game? Good for you! Unfortunately, copyright does not protect the idea for a game, its name or title, the way it's played (called "game mechanics" in the law), or your marketing ideas. You can copyright the design of the board art, the playing pieces, and written rules.[108]

Once a game has been made public, nothing prevents others from developing a game based on similar principles. They just

---

[105] US Copyright Office, *Compendium*, Chapter 900: Visual Art Works, § 906.4 (rev'd 2021)
[106] *Id.*
[107] *Id.*
[108] US Copyright Office, Document fl-108 (rev'd 2016) The Copyright Office recommends that you apply to register a game with written rules as a literary work.

can't copy the art on your board or your specific rules or the design of your playing pieces.

There are limits to the protection copyright law provides for a board game. However, the name of your board game, and any logos, symbols, or artwork associated with it, may be protectable under trademark law. You can also explore patenting your game.

Game Design

The copyrightable elements of a game may include text, artwork, sound recordings, and/or audiovisual material. These elements may be protectable if they contain a sufficient amount of original authorship.[109]

Elements of game design that *aren't* copyrightable include the basic idea for a game and the rules for playing and scoring a game. These elements cannot be registered, regardless of how unique, clever, or fun they may be. If you're registering a copyright in a game, you can describe the text, artwork on a playing board, and any original sculptural elements of game pieces.

GRAFFITI

The basic rule is, don't spray paint stuff on other people's property. That's generally considered vandalism and you shouldn't do it.

Now that we've got that out of the way, let's consider the copyright issues involved with street art, otherwise known as graffiti. Graffiti is a "subversive" art form: by its very nature it demands that its artists vandalize public or private property. Whether it's a middle schooler tagging the back of a store with their name, a muralist creating a vibrant landscape on an overpass, or Banksy spray painting valuable artworks on the

---

[109] US Copyright Office, *Compendium*, Chapter 900: Games, § 910 (rev'd 2021)

side of someone's garage, it's pretty much not graffiti unless its "canvas" belongs to someone else. And that's the trouble.

Certainly graffiti is protectable by copyright. It is a "pictorial or graphic" "original work of authorship" that is "fixed in any tangible medium of expression" from which it "can be perceived."[110] So it satisfies the copyright statute's requirements for protection. Like any other original work, copyright happens automatically, as soon as the artist has emptied their last can of spray paint. Because there's no provision in the Copyright Act saying that it can't be registered, presumably the Copyright Office would approve registration of a graffiti artist's copyright application.

There are some interesting questions in this area though, most of which unfortunately don't have answers yet, and so fall into the bucket of "things you need to think about carefully." First, if the graffiti is on a public building or otherwise freely visible by the public, how protected can it be against people photographing it, or accidentally including it in a panning shot in a movie? Second, if the graffiti image is affixed to a privately-owned building, who owns the art: the artist or the person who owns its canvas?

There have been a few cases that provide some—but not much—guidance. In one case, the clothing chain H&M used a graffitied wall in a public park as the background for an advertising photoshoot. The graffiti artist sent H&M a cease-and-desist letter, claiming copyright infringement. H&M sought a court order that graffiti was per se not copyrightable because it is illegally installed on property. We'll never know how the court would have decided that case, because the loud public outcry from graffiti artists and their allies caused H&M to drop the lawsuit and the ad campaign.

---

[110] 17 USC § 102

In another case, a graffiti artist sued HBO for airing an episode of the series, *Vinyl*, in which a character walks past the artist's work on a dumpster in the street.[111] The artist claimed that "HBO depicted the graffiti "without permission, compensation, or attribution" and thus infringed his copyright and trademark rights."[112]

The court disagreed, on the basis that Gayle's claims

> are premised on a fleeting shot of barely visible graffiti painted on what appears to be a dumpster in the background of a single scene. The overall scene is brief, and the graffiti at issue appears on screen for no more than two to three seconds. ... Moreover, the graffiti is never pictured "by itself or in a close-up," and it plays absolutely no "role in the plot.". Instead, the camera is focused on the actress in the foreground, who is well-lit and depicted in an eye-catching bright-red dress. By contrast, the graffiti is, at best, shown in the background at an oblique angle and in low, uneven light such that it is "never fully visible," let alone legible. ... In short, the graffiti "was filmed in such a manner and appears so fleetingly that ... there is no plausible claim for copyright infringement here."[113]

Finally, in what is known as "The 5Pointz Litigation,"[114] 21 graffiti artists (referred to by the court as "aerosol artists") sued a real estate developer to stop his planned demolition of a warehouse on which their works were displayed. During earlier litigation, the developer ignored a pending court decision on an injunction to delay the demolition pending trial, and whitewashed the images, effectively destroying them as much as knocking down the building would. The court took a dim view

---

[111] Gayle v. HBO, Inc. - No. 17-CV-5867 (JMF). (S.D.N.Y. 2018)
[112] *Id.*
[113] *Id.*, citing Gottlieb v Paramount, 590 F. Supp. 2d at 634 (SDNY 2008)
[114] Cohen, et. al., v G&M Realty Inc, 320 F. Supp. 3d 421, 447 (EDN, 2018).

of the developer's attitude, and ultimately found in favor of the artists under copyright law and the Visual Artists Right Act (VARA) (see "Paintings & Sculptures" in Chapter 5 for more detail on VARA). The court fined the developer over $6,750,000 in statutory damages, divided among the artists on the basis of how much of their work had been destroyed.[115] (The judge observed that "If not for [the developer's] insolence, these damages would not have been assessed," and "The shame of it all is that since 5Pointz was a prominent tourist attraction the public would undoubtedly have thronged to say its goodbyes during those 10 months and gaze at the formidable works of aerosol art for the last time. It would have been a wonderful tribute for the artists that they richly deserved."[116] The developer appealed the decision to the US Supreme Court, which refused to hear the case, leaving the decision—and the fines—intact.

GRAPHIC DESIGN

Graphic design is the use of shape, color, space, form, line, value, and texture to communicate information, often commercially. Because its function is to convey information rather than to elicit an emotional or aesthetic response, graphic design is a distinct creative field from painting or other graphic arts. Two-dimensional graphic designs are generally protectable by copyright if they are original and "separable from the utilitarian aspects"—that is separate from the function of—whatever they are applied to (fabrics, wallpaper, containers, etc.).[117]

TATTOOS

The question of tattoos and copyright is a little murky. There have been no federal court decisions one way or the other

---

[115] *Id.*

[116] *Id.*

[117] US Copyright Office, *Compendium*, Chapter 900: Jewelry, §§ 913, 920.2 (rev'd 2021)

(although *Whitmill* comes close, as we'll see shortly). Technically, tattoos seem to fall neatly under the basic definition of copyright protection in 17 USC§ 102:

> "Copyright protection subsists... in original works of authorship fixed in any tangible medium of expression, now known or later developed, from which they can be perceived, reproduced, or otherwise communicated, either directly or with the aid of a machine or device."[118]

A tattoo can certainly be perceived (seen). On the other hand, much like the challenge faced by Chapman Kelley in *Kelley v. Chicago Park District*, it's conceivable that a question could be raised about whether human flesh (the cells of which continually slough off and are replaced) is not "fixed" much like plants in a garden.[119]

The main question with tattoos, though, is whether or not a tattoo is an "original work of authorship" under the statute *once it's on someone's skin*. That is, who "owns" the tattoo: the person whose skin it's on, or the person who created the design? The design of the tattoo—the artwork on paper—is certainly copyrightable, as long as it meets the statute's criteria for originality, isn't derivative or infringing on an existing design, and meets the Copyright Office's expectations for complexity and uniqueness.

The basic rule, though, appears to be that the tattoo artist owns the copyright to the design, regardless of whose skin the tattoo is on. If someone sees a tattoo on someone, takes a picture of it, and asks another artist to reproduce it, the original artist's copyright is being violated. Of course, the First Sale Doctrine allows the tattooed person to have the tattoo modified or

---

[118] 17 USC § 102
[119] It should be noted, though, that it is the epidermis—the top layer of skin—that is continually replacing itself; tattoo ink is generally applied to the dermis, the layer of skin beneath the epidermis, which organically replaces itself much more slowly.

covered or removed entirely. But they have no rights to the underlying design; that belongs to the artist.

 The closest we've gotten to a resolution of the tattoo/copyright question is a case involving the 2011 movie, *The Hangover Part II*. [120] In the movie, a character wakes up after a night of drunken partying in Bangkok to find a tribal tattoo around his left eye, his skin still painfully pink. The tattoo is identical to Mike Tyson's (a reference to the boxer's cameo in the original 2009 movie).

Tyson's tattoo artist, S. Victor Whitmill, filed a lawsuit against Warner Bros. Entertainment just weeks before the movie's premier. Since he held a copyright for the eight-year-old artwork, he claimed that the use of his design in the movie and in advertisements without his consent was copyright infringement and sought an injunction against the movie's release. Warner Bros. argued that it was an acceptable use.

The judge noted that the facts were uncontested:

- Whitmill created the tattoo on Tyson's face, and Tyson signed a release of all ownership in the design to Whitmill. Whitmill was the copyright owner.
- Neither Tyson nor Warner Bros. sought permission from Whitmill to use the tattoo, either in *Hangover I* or *II*.
- *Hangover I* showed only Tyson's face and did not use the tattoo apart from his face. *Hangover II* was a non-Tyson use of the tattoo, using the tattoo on another character's face in a majority of the scenes in the movie. However, the tattoo is insignificant to the plot line.
- Warner Bros. has spent millions promoting the film and its scheduled opening.

---

[120] *Whitmill v. Warner Bros.* Entertainment Inc., 4:11-cv-00752 (E.D. Mo., 2011)

The judge also made the following legal observations:

- Whitmill's likelihood of prevailing was "strong" and Warner Bros' arguments were "silly."
- Warner Bros' use of the tattoo was unauthorized. The tattoo as a plot device could have been replaced with any other tattoo. The copy was exact.

The judge then proceeded to decide the case in favor of Warner Bros.

Wait, what?

Balancing the equities (that is, thinking about who *should* win in fairness v. who *would* win under law) the judge described the harm to Warner Bros as "very large" and Whitmill's harm comparatively small:

- Warner Brothers would lose millions of dollars if the movie was delayed for trial;
- Whitmill was losing control of his art, but Warner Bros would potentially lose a lot of money;
- It was only one tattoo design, without significant effect on the Whitmill's business;
- The "public interest" in seeing *The Hangover II* was strong. If the movie was not released, theatre owners and distributors would lose a lot of money, too.

So unfortunately, in one of the few tattoo cases we have, profit won over an artist's rights. On the other hand, the case never went to trial, where the copyright question would have probably been resolved in Whitmill's favor, because the parties reached an out of court settlement on their own.

So what do you take away from all this? Four simple points to remember:

1. Characters are considered media-neutral under copyright law, so it doesn't matter if your character is drawn for a book or animation.
2. A game's idea, name or title, and rules are not copyrightable. But you can copyright the design of the board art, the playing pieces, and written rules, especially if they're stated creatively.
3. The design of a tattoo is copyrighted by the artist, and copying an existing tattoo from someone's shoulder (or face) is infringement of the original artist's copyright.
4. The simple and commercial nature of traditional graphic design may make it difficult to copyright.

Chapter 6
Music

MUSICAL COMPOSITIONS

Musical compositions are explicitly protected by copyright under the Copyright Law.[121] The statutory phrase, "musical works, including any accompanying words," includes both compositions and performances (see below), as long as they are fixed in a tangible form of expression.

Under copyright, then, composers have exactly the same rights in their works as anyone else: the right to make copies, to create derivative works, to sell or distribute copies, to display the work, and to perform the work publicly. The copyright in a musical composition also includes the right to make or authorize the first sound recording of the composition—a right that includes the rights of performance and distribution.

As a general rule, the composer always retains copyright to a musical work, regardless of who performs or covers it. And as with any other form of copyrightable creative work, the composer can license any of those rights to other people on any terms they like.

---

[121] 17 USC § 102(a)(2)

Statutory License

There is one unique copyright twist for musical compositions, however: the *statutory license*, also known as a *compulsory* or *mechanical license*. As we've learned, normally a copyright holder can decide whether or not to grant other people permission to perform their work. But for musical compositions, the law has established a requirement that once a composer has published or performed a composition, they *must* allow others to perform the work, as long as a royalty is paid to the composer and other requirements are met.[122] The statutory license also allows licensees to introduce a different musical arrangement of the work to accommodate the style of the performance. (For example, if someone wanted to produce a recording of Cardi B's song, "WAP" using Baroque instruments and an AI-synthesized vocal.)

You don't have to use the statutory license; you can of course negotiate directly with the copyright owner for a grant of rights (called a "voluntary license" to distinguish it from statutory). But if the copyright holder doesn't want to negotiate with you, the statutory license ensures that you can make your recording anyway, as long as you pay the statutory license.[123]

A person claiming a statutory license must also demonstrate to the Copyright Office that

- Their purpose is to distribute phonorecords of sound recordings to the public for private use; and
- The musical composition has already been recorded and distributed by the copyright holder

The current statutory license royalty rate, established by the Copyright Office's Copyright Royalty Judges, is 15.1% (for context, note that in 2018 the rate was 11.1%, so it reflects cost

---

[122] 17 USC § 115
[123] US Copyright Office, Circular 73 (rev'd 2018)

of living or inflationary pressures).[124] As a result of 2018's Music Modernization Act, the US Copyright Office designated the Mechanical Licensing Collective (MLC) to collect and distribute mechanical royalty payments as required by the new statute. Songwriters and music publishers are now required to register with MLC using its online portal to receive royalty payments under the statutory license.[125]

Much of this discussion is focused on using other people's music. But if you're a songwriter or composer, be sure to take advantage of the opportunities offered by the Music Modernization Act to protect your copyright and potentially receive additional income.

The owner of a song's copyright *must* grant you a statutory license if you pay the royalty fee. But the statutory license only covers the audio version. If you want to produce and publicly display a video with your song, you'll need to obtain a **synchronization license**, or "sync license." Sync licenses are not statutory, and must be negotiated directly with the copyright owner (or their representative). Unlike statutory licenses, though, there is no requirement that a copyright holder grant you a sync license.

MUSICAL PERFORMANCES

A musical composition is not the same as a musical performance or recording. When you write music, your song is protected by copyright just like any other work that's written down. When you record a song, you're creating both a musical work and a sound recording. A sound recording and the music, lyrics, words, or other content included in the recording are separate copyright-protected works that need to be registered separately.

---

[124] 84 FR 1918 (2019)
[125] US Copyright Office, "Music Modernization Act" (www.copyright.gov/music-modernization/)

According to the US Copyright Office, a public performance of a musical work does not necessarily constitute publication. "Publication" is a very specific thing that occurs on the date on which *copies* of the work are first made available to the public.[126] A "performance" is any display of a work "at a place open to the public or at any place where a substantial number of persons outside of a normal circle of a family and...social acquaintances is gathered," or to transmit or otherwise communicate a performance or display of the work to a specific place or to the public generally, whether or not they're in the same location.[127] That is, to broadcast or stream a performance is to "perform it."

Usually, venues that host live performances of cover versions—bars, restaurants, festivals, etc.—already have arrangements with a performance rights organization (PRO) such as Harry Fox, Sound Exchange, BMI, ASCAP or SESAC to cover statutory licenses, so performers don't need to worry about it. They royalties are based on revenue generated by the performance: a percentage of the cover charge, food and beverage revenue, etc. Representatives of PROs often make secret visits to venues to ensure that all live covers (and recorded music) is properly accounted for. Make sure your venue has a license, though, before performing your cover versions in public: while PROs generally deal with venues (because they usually have deeper pockets), they can and do sometimes pursue unlicensed performers.

MUSICAL RECORDINGS

A musical composition is the collection of notes and instructions that define a musical work. A musical *recording*[128] is "a series of musical, spoken, or other sounds fixed in a recording

---

[126] US Copyright Office, *Compendium*, Chapter 1900: Publication, § 1902 (rev'd 2021)
[127] 17 USC § 101
[128] Although we're focused on music here, the same copyright principles cover all sorts of sound recordings.

medium"[129] such as vinyl, CD, tape, or digital media. Collectively, those media are referred to in copyright law as "phonorecords." The "author" of a musical recording can be the composer (in the case of singer-songwriters, for instance), or a music producer, or someone else. If you're the "someone else" who isn't the composer, then you'll need to either have the composer's permission to make a recording, or rely on the statutory license discussed above, or risk a lawsuit for copyright infringement.

The recording of a musical composition may have multiple copyright holders, depending on the relationship among the composer, singers, musicians, and producers—for instance, if you compose a song, but during the recording process the performer and producer work with you to alter it, they can claim copyright as well.[130] The ownership of copyright should be clearly established prior to creating the recording, to avoid conflicts later, and any permissions granted by a composer to others should be crystal clear about what rights are being granted and what rights are being retained.

A **cover version** of a song is where a singer or musician makes their own version of an original song composed and performed by someone else. Sometimes, the goal is to sound as much like the original as possible (as is the case with "tribute bands" that adopt the sound, style, and look of the original performers of the music). Other times, artists are putting old wine in a new bottle by putting their own unique stylistic spin on someone else's song, bringing a new interpretation of the composition. Cover versions can be either performances or recordings or both. Sometimes cover versions are even more popular than the originals:

---

[129] US Copyright Office, "Musical Works, Sound Recordings & Copyright" (rev'd 2020)

[130] That's why when a song wins an award, you'll frequently see multiple people going up to the stage to accept it: they all own part of the song, either through participation in its composing or by contractual agreement.

- "All Along the Watchtower" by Jimi Hendrix (originally recorded by Bob Dylan)

- "Hallelujah" by Jeff Buckley (originally recorded by Leonard Cohen)

- "I Will Always Love You" by Whitney Houston (originally recorded by Dolly Parton).[131]

When you are recording a cover version of someone else's copyrighted music, you can provide notice of a statutory license and pay the license fees through one of several performance rights organizations (PROs) that handle statutory royalties, such as Harry Fox, Sound Exchange, BMI, ASCAP or SESAC. These PROs obtain rights from copyright holders, and act on their behalf to enforce and collect royalties.

Some social media platforms, internet radio, and non-interactive webcasts usually have statutory license arrangements in place so they can stream cover versions—for instance YouTube shares ad revenue with copyright holders.

MUSICAL SAMPLING

Sampling is the use of other, preexisting sound recordings to add depth or texture or even commentary to a musical composition. Those recordings can be of music, speech, or sounds. For example, here are some well-known songs that include sampling:

- Ava Max's "Kings & Queens" samples from Bonnie Tyler's "If You Were A Woman"
- Billie Eilish's "my strange addiction" samples from an episode of "The Office" (Eilish also used the sounds of Australian pedestrian crosswalk signals in "Bad Guy")

---

[131] US Copyright Office, "Sampling, Interpolations, Beat Stores and More" (rev'd 2021)

- Charli XCX's "Boys" samples a coin sound from the Super Mario Bros. game
- Doja Cat's "Kiss Me More" samples from Olivia Newton-John's "Physical"
- Kanye West's "Blood on the Leaves" samples from Nina Simone's cover of Billie Holiday's "Strange Fruit" (Ye also sampled Daft Punk's "Harder, Better, Faster, Stronger" in "Stronger")
- Lady Gaga's "Babylon" sampled bird songs and wind chimes (Gaga also sampled Queen's "We Will Rock You" in "Yoü and I")
- Lil Nas X's "Industry Baby" samples from Rowdy Rebel's "Computers"
- M.I.A.'s "Paper Planes" samples from The Clash's "Straight to Hell"
- Madonna's "Hung Up" samples from ABBA's "Gimme Gimme Gimme" (and Cher's cover of "Gimme Gimme Gimme" includes samples from "Hung Up").

There's nothing wrong with sampling; it provides musicians with the opportunity to make ironic comment on their own or others' songs, and to give greater interest or depth to their music. Sampling in most cases is a "transformative use" of the original recording, since samples are often manipulated or altered to fit the musical tone and style of the new recording.

Remember that when you're sampling a song, you're not sampling the composition, but a sound recording of the composition—they're two separate things. A musical work is a song's composition and lyrics as created by a composer. A sound recording is a collection of sounds fixed in a physical or digital recording medium.

There are other ways of including other music in a recording. These include mashups, remixes, and interpolations.

A **mashup** is where a musician combines two existing musical samples into a single one. For instance, the TV series *Glee* was famous for creating mashups, such as Elton John's "The Bitch Is Back" combined with Madonna's "Dress You Up." Mashups are similar to medleys—where one song flows into another one—but usually in a mashup there's additional original material included or created as a result of the combined musical works.

A **remix** is where a musician takes an existing sound recording and manipulates it, adding additional digital or analog instrumentation, different beats, or changing the song's speed. Remixes are especially common in electronic and dance music, where songs are often enhanced and sped up to create dance versions of pop songs or ballads. For instance, in 2020 Lady Gaga released her "Chromatica" album, and in 2021 released a version of the album's songs remixed by other DJs and performers as "Dawn of Chromatica."

An **interpolation** is trickier. While sampling, mashups, and remixes all rely on a sound recording, an interpolation involves taking the original composition and combining it with a new work. That is, the musician is not using a prerecorded musical piece as part of their music, they're using the original composition—the musical notation or "sheet music" itself—to create a new work. For example, Flo Rida's "Right Round" interpolates Dead or Alive's "You Spin Me Round" and Ariana Grande's "7 Rings" interpolates "My Favorite Things" from Rodgers and Hammerstein's "Sound of Music." In that case, Ariana isn't sampling a soundtrack recording of Julie Andrews singing about raindrops on roses and whiskers on kittens; she's using Rodgers and Hammerstein's composition and making it a part of her song.

Sampling and Copyright Law

Any use of someone else's copyrighted music without permission —whether the whole song or just a brief snippet— is copyright infringement and exposes you to a costly lawsuit. That's the general rule to remember. Period.

What's more, unlike obtaining a license to create a cover version, there is no statutory license that requires a copyright holder to allow sampling. To obtain permission to use all or part of someone's copyrighted music, you'll need to contact the copyright holder. Figuring out who that is can be tricky, but a good place to start is by looking at the Song Credits list on Spotify or the liner credits on a CD or vinyl. The Internet also has the answers to many questions. Also, be prepared: most copyright holders will expect compensation for the sampling, including advance payments and a royalty percentage, and there's no statutory requirement that limits how much compensation an artist expects—or that they give you permission in exchange for any level of compensation.

Remember that all these rules and requirements work both ways, though. If you're a songwriter or composer, and someone wants to sample your music, you are as entitled as anyone else to set your compensation requirements. It's your copyright, after all.

But keep in mind what we talked about earlier in this book: there are some affirmative defenses to infringement that are highly relevant here. Fair use is the primary one. As has been suggested earlier, sampling can be transformative, critical, or even satirical. Since all three of those things fall comfortably under fair use, there may not be an issue with your sampling resulting in a court finding you guilty of infringement.

It's always the better practice, though, to not count on a future legal outcome; judges or juries may not see things quite the same way you do, and in any case a lawsuit is a costly, time-consuming, and stressful thing to deal with. Even if you think your sampling clearly constitutes fair use, your best bet is to obtain permission, and not use the sample if you can't get it.

For this case study, I'm providing sort of a "sampling sampler:" three snapshots of some famous sampling cases: one that

found no infringement, one that was settled out of court, and one that found quite a bit of infringement.

Campbell v. Acuff-Rose Music.[132] Acuff-Rose Music filed suit against the members of the rap group 2 Live Crew and their record company, claiming that 2 Live Crew's 1989 song, "Pretty Woman," infringed Acuff-Rose's copyright in Roy Orbison's 1964 rock ballad, "Oh, Pretty Woman." The case made it to the US Supreme Court, which held that the use constituted parody. Justice Souter wrote, "Even if 2 Live Crew's copying of the original's first line of lyrics and characteristic opening bass riff may be said to go to the original's "heart," that heart is what most readily conjures up the song for parody, and it is the heart at which parody takes aim. Moreover, 2 Live Crew thereafter departed markedly from the Orbison lyrics and produced otherwise distinctive music."

David Bowie and Queen v. Vanilla Ice (1990) This infringement case was settled out of court without a lawsuit. Basically, Bowie and Queen sued rapper Vanilla Ice for his use of the instantly-recognizable bass line from their copyrighted 1981 song, "Under Pressure." The parties came to an agreement under which Ice would pay Bowie and Queen a royalty on sales of his song. Ice later paid Bowie and Queen $4 million to acquire the rights to "Under Pressure" entirely, mostly to avoid paying royalties forever.[133]

Pharrell Williams and Robin Thicke v. Frankie Gaye.[134] Pharrell Williams and Robin Thicke's 2013 song "Blurred Lines" (named Billboard's Song of the Summer) was found to have borrowed heavily from Marvin Gaye's 1977 song, "Got To Give It Up." A jury awarded the Gaye estate $5.3 million and a perpetual 50% royalty on sales of "Blurred Lines." On appeal

---

[132] 510 US 569 (1994)
[133] Vondran, Steve, "Five Important Music Infringement Cases Deal with Mixing/Sampling" (2021) https://www.vondranlegal.com/five-music-infringement-cases-mixingsampling
[134] No. 15-56880 (9th Cir. 2018)

(which upheld the verdict), the court applied two tests: an objective "extrinsic test" that relies on expert testimony to dissect and analyze the structure of the two compositions; and a subjective intrinsic test, that asks "whether the ordinary, reasonable person would find the total concept and feel of the works to be substantially similar."[135]

Contrary to popular belief, **there is no 6-Second Rule** *(or 10-Second Rule, or 30-Second Rule or any other Rule) for how much of a copyrighted song someone can "legally" infringe before they can be sued. If a one-second snippet is identifiable as coming from someone's copyrighted work, it's infringement. Don't take other people's stuff.*

 So what do you take away from all this? Four simple points to remember:

1. Musical compositions are explicitly protected by copyright under the Copyright Law.
2. "Statutory licenses" are a legal requirement that once a composer has published or performed a composition, they *must* allow others to perform the work, as long as a royalty is paid to the composer and other requirements are met.
3. In most cases, sampling is a "transformative use" of the original recorded sound, if the sample is manipulated or altered to fit the new recording.
4. There is no minimum snippet of sound that is OK to infringe. If the snippet is identifiable as someone else's copyrighted work, it's infringement—although of course an affirmative defense may apply.

---

[135] *Id.*

Chapter 7
Needlework & Clothing

CLOTHING

A "useful article" is an article having an intrinsic utilitarian function that is not merely to portray the appearance of the article or to convey information. An article that is normally a part of a useful article is considered a "useful article"[136]—that is, sofa cushions are considered part of a sofa; a tablecloth or placemats are useful items; and, as a general rule, clothing is a very useful item indeed for most of us. So the general rule is that clothing cannot be copyrighted.

Although copyright may not protect "useful articles" of clothing, trademark law may offer a good alternative for clothing designers to find some protections. Trademark law will protect your logo or other identifying features (including colors that are closely associated with your brand—think of Louis Vuitton red on the soles of women's shoes). That's why you often see designer clothing that's a mass of the designer's logo, or designer logos prominently featured on other articles, like handbags or sunglasses; it has the effect of deterring copying like copyright

---

[136] 17 US C. § 101

would, because to duplicate the item the infringer needs to duplicate the trademark, and that's a very bad thing to do.

That said, there are (because this is law) some exceptions to that rule. For instance, you can copyright your sketches of a fashion design, and copyright law will protect those sketches *as drawings*. What the law won't protect is the *idea* of the clothing in your sketches. So your drawing of a conceptual pantsuit is protected, but nothing really stops Armani or Dior from making an actual pantsuit that looks a lot like your artwork.

Speaking of artwork, if you create original, unique art that you apply to fabrics, your imprinted design may be protected by copyright. Of course, clothing made with that imprinted fabric won't be protected, but the fabric design is.

As the US Supreme Court put it: "[A] feature incorporated into the design of a useful article is eligible for copyright protection only if the feature

(1) can be perceived as a two- or three-dimensional work of art separate from the useful article and

(2) would qualify as a protectable pictorial, graphic, or sculptural work...if it were imagined separately from the useful article into which it is incorporated."[137]

Ⓒase Study A company called Varsity Brands designed, manufactured, and sold cheerleading uniforms. They held more than 200 copyrights on two-dimensional designs that appeared on their uniforms, primarily combinations, positionings, and arrangements of elements that include "lines, curves, stripes, angles, diagonals, chevrons, coloring, and shapes."[138] Another company, Star Athletica, also marketed and sold cheerleading

---

[137] *Star Athletica, LLC, v. Varsity Brands, Inc.*, 137 S.Ct. 1002 (2017)
[138] *Id.*

uniforms, and Varsity sued them for infringing on their copyrights for five designs. (*See illustration 1*)

Illustration 1[139]

The trial court ruled for Star Athletica, because the designs did not qualify as "protectable pictorial, graphic, or sculptural works [because they] served the useful or utilitarian function of identifying the garments as cheerleading uniforms and therefore could not be physically or conceptually separated from the uniform's utilitarian function."[140]

The US Supreme Court disagreed, holding that under the copyright statute, "a useful article is eligible for copyright if, when identified and imagined apart from the useful article, it would qualify as a pictorial, graphic, or sculptural work either on its own or when fixed in some other tangible medium."[141] Here, the Court reasoned, the designs could be removed from the cheerleading uniforms and applied to other media—for instance, hung on the wall as team banners. What's really significant here is that the Supreme Court said very clearly that it didn't matter if, after removing the copyrightable components, there was nothing left of the functional item.

---

[139] *Id.*, Appendix to the Opinion of the Court
[140] *Id.*
[141] *Id.*

The "separability doctrine" means that as long as designs can be separated from their functional home and used in a more conceptually "artistic" way, they can be protected by copyright.

COSTUMES

So, clothing is obviously a useful article, but *costumes* are different, right? Well, surprisingly, not so much. Remember that a "useful article" is legally defined as having "an intrinsic utilitarian function that is not merely to portray the appearance of the article or to convey information."[142] Generally, courts (and the Copyright Office) have held that costumes are pretty much just another kind of clothing, and just as much a useful article as any old pair of jeans.

"But," you say, "a costume is clearly a creative work, because it takes imagination and creativity to produce something that lets the wearer look like a witch or a fairy princess or a pumpkin or Captain Amazing!" Well that's true, but here's what one court said, which pretty much summarizes the general opinion of American courts on the question of costume copyrightability:

> The artistic features of the various costumes — the elaborate headpieces on the Hippo Ballerina, T-Rex or Jack O'Lantern, for example, or the orange gingham print on the Jack O'Lantern, or the attractive color combinations and facial details on all the costumes — all are influenced by, and indeed advance, the utilitarian purpose of the items, which is to enable the wearer to masquerade.[143]

---

[142] 17 USC § 101

[143] *Whimsicality, Inc. v Rubie's Costumes Co, Inc.*, 721 F.Supp. 1566 (1989). It's worth noting that in *Whimsicality*, the plaintiff didn't help their case by trying to trick the Copyright Office in their copyright application. Knowing that defining their work as costumes would result in a denial of copyright on the basis of the useful article doctrine, the plaintiffs described them instead as fabric "soft sculptures...*adaptable*

That is, something is a useful article, or "utilitarian," if it serves a specific useful purpose. However whimsical, the specific useful purpose of a costume is to make the wearer look like someone or something else. So if the costume is successful, it is by definition a useful article.

Masks, however, seem to be more acceptable to the Copyright Office and courts as "sculptural works."

But all is not entirely lost. Drawings of a costume—as well as graphic depictions of scenery, sets, props, lighting, makeup, and other elements of stagecraft—may be included in the copyright application of the underlying dramatic work. You can copyright a play, and if your play includes descriptions and illustrations of technical elements (scenery, sets, props, makeup, lighting, etc.) then those illustrations and descriptions are copyrightable. But ironically the actual technical elements themselves, when put on a stage, are not copyrightable.

NEEDLEWORK, FABRICS & QUILTS

As a general rule, useful items are not copyrightable. "Useful items" include clothing, blankets, bedspreads, curtains, rugs, doorknobs, furniture—anything with a utilitarian use, regardless of how original or artistic it is. Here, we're using the term "needlework" to refer to pretty much anything that's produced using a needle, thread, and fabric. Generally, such items are based on patterns, and there's a whole section on those below.

Creative works made out of cloth are a mixed bag in terms of copyright. As discussed earlier, clothing—a "useful item" for most of us—is not copyrightable. The fabrics used to make

---

for use as costumes, wall hangings or interior decorations." [emphasis added] All of Whimsicality's catalogs and advertising, however, referred to their products only as costumes. *Id.*

clothing, however, may be copyrighted if they display sufficient uniqueness and creativity to qualify as "works of authorship."

If you're making things out of fabric that you've woven yourself, using wool from your own sheep or cotton from your own fields, and natural dyes made from berries in your own orchard, then you have no copyright concerns other than protecting your own work. Congratulations!

Unfortunately, most people will be using commercially-available, pre-printed fabrics, and that's where there's a wrinkle: Those fabrics are very likely under copyright.[144] Now you're in a pickle, right?

You'll recall that there is a thing called the *First Sale Doctrine*. To briefly recap, the First Sale Doctrine means that if you buy a copyrighted work, you have the right to do what you want with it—burn it, give it away, make it into origami doves, or even sell it. (That's why there are so many used books for sale on eBay; it's perfectly OK to sell someone else's copyrighted work if you've legitimately purchased a copy.)

You should also remember that there's also something called *Transformative Use*, which means that your infringement of someone else's copyright is OK if the result transforms the copyrighted work into something new.

So you go to The Fabric Store and you buy twenty yards of cotton jersey that is printed with Donald Duck's face. You proceed to make ten beautiful tee shirts out of the fabric (using your own pattern) and sell them on your website. Can you expect a nasty letter from Disney? The answer is probably not, because of those two principles: first sale and transformative use. Let's break it down.

First, you purchased the jersey at The Fabric Store and now those twenty yards are yours to do with as you like, under the

---

[144] The copyright notice on bulk fabric is usually printed along the selvage.

First Sale Doctrine. In addition, you purchased a single long piece of fabric, and you've transformed it into tee shirts. That's a pretty transformative use.

Of course, you can also contact the copyright holder for permission. (Having a lawyer help you with that isn't a bad idea.) But be prepared: the copyright holder is unlikely to just say "OK have fun!" Instead, they're just as likely to either refuse permission altogether or demand either a license fee or royalty on sales, or both. Your best bet is to put your own imagination to work and come up with your own original prints and designs, or to use printed fabrics that are in the public domain.

Here's a real-life example. My friend Marie makes beautiful textile collages, cloth decoupage, and artfully dyed fabric panels. Recently she decided to do interpretations of paintings as fabric collages, and made the mistake of asking me if that was OK. You can probably guess the answer: unless the inspiring artist's work is in the public domain (I'm looking at you, Mona Lisa), my friend's "interpretations" are simply derivative works, produced without permission, that don't fall into the fair use categories. Just because Paul Klee never made a fabric collage version of "Twittering Machine" or "Castle and Sun" doesn't mean he doesn't still have the right to do it (well, in Klee's case it's his estate that holds copyright until 70 years after the date of his death, so it's their decision to make). There's a happy ending to this story, though: because Paul Klee died in 1940 (that's not the happy part, obviously) the copyright on his work expired in the US 70 years later, or 2010. So Marie is in luck!

Quilts are interesting, in general and in copyright terms. First, everything said about **patterns** in the following section applies, obviously, to quilts and quilt patterns. If you're making and selling patchwork quilts, you still need to be mindful of any copyrighted or trademarked fabrics in the mix, even though you're only using small pieces. So, for instance, a pop culture-themed quilt using swatches of children's bedsheets depicting Disney, Star Wars, and Marvel characters and properties might be fine as a cherished family heirloom, but it cannot be mass-produced or sold to the public without risking the appearance of unfriendly cease-and-desist letters from IP attorneys.

ⓒase Study Thimbleberries, Inc. designs and sells quilt patterns in shops and through books and magazines. [145] One of those patterns is called "Countryside Wreath." When Thimbleberries' owner and chief designer saw the Countryside Wreath printed on tablecloths and table runners in a Charles Keath catalog, she immediately demanded they cease and desist. Keath (and C&F Enterprises, which manufactures the table linens) refused. The court found that while Thimbleberries was not entitled to a monopoly on the concept of arranging squares and triangles in a wreath-shaped pattern, their design nonetheless was one unique example of the many possible ways of doing that, and so was not subject to the *scenes a faire* doctrine we talked about before—that is, there were so many ways to arrange triangles and squares in a wreathlike pattern that Thimbleberries' design was not required by the genre.

The court then applied a two-part test for copying. First, it did an *extrinsic test*: looking to see if, in general, the two designs were similar. Finding that they were, it moved to an intrinsic test: looking more closely to determine if a reasonable person, through normal observation, would be able to tell the difference between the two designs. The court concluded:

> *To the ordinary observer, the two designs are, for all practical purposes, identical: the shapes of the designs are identical, consisting of sixteen exterior points of 45 degrees and six exterior points of 90 degrees; the number and placement of squares and triangles is virtually the same, except for four triangular pieces flanking the contrasting bow which have been removed from the*

---

[145] *Thimbleberries, Inc. v. C & F Enterprises*, 142 F. Supp. 2d 1132 - Dist. Court, Minnesota 2001.

> *defendants' design; and finally, the number of pieces, their scale and the proportions used in both designs are identical. For example, both patterns utilize six square pieces and eight triangular pieces, arranged the same way, to comprise the bow, which is placed in the identical location on the wreath. Most telling is the nearly identical arrangement of squares and triangles to create both the exterior shape of the wreath and the center hole design. The striking similarities between these two works stands in sharp contrast to the notably different wreath patterns created by other quilt pattern designers.*[146]

The court granted Thimbleberries' motion for a preliminary injunction to stop C&F from manufacturing, and Keath from selling, the wreath table linens.

PATTERNS

Because a pattern is a set of instructions on how to make something, it isn't copyrightable. [147] That's because instructions, recipes, assembly directions, etc. are explicitly excluded from copyright protection. However—and this is a big "however"—anything that's unique about the patterns, such as how they're drawn or descriptive text, *is* copyrightable. That's a pretty vague line between ok and not ok, and your best bet is to err on the side of assuming that anything you create from a pattern is a permitted (even expected) derivative use done with the implied permission of the copyright holder.

But that implied permission has limits: it assumes that the item will be made for personal use rather than commercial production and distribution. Any use other than "personal use" may be a violation of the pattern artist's copyright.

So let's make this personal: If the patterns being published are yours, you should expect that people will use them to create

---

[146] *Id.*
[147] 17 USC § 113(b)

clothing (or whatever they're patterns for). You may even expect that people will copy your patterns onto larger sheets of paper to make the process easier, or may photocopy the patterns directly from your book. You should expect that people will make the items you've created patterns for, and will display or wear them. You might be OK with people who make, say, a skirt from one of your patterns selling that skirt at a community arts and crafts fair. However, you would certainly *not* be OK with Yves Saint Laurent buying a copy of your pattern book and then mass-producing a skirt based on your pattern and selling it in high-end boutiques on Rodeo Drive or Fifth Avenue.

To recap: Photocopying or otherwise reproducing patterns from a pattern book is, technically, a copyright violation. Producing the item for which the patterns are intended is not a copyright violation. Selling the item on a mass scale may a violation of copyright.

Licensing

Typically, you'll find language like this in a pattern book:

> *[Publisher and/or Designer] grants you a limited license to produce a derivative work from the designs published in this collection, subject to two strict limitations: (1) Such derivative work may be for personal use only (that is, not for commercial resale); and (2) no more than one (1) derivative work may be produced from any single design included in this publication. Any commercial or mass-production of works based wholly or partially on the designs contained here is absolutely forbidden without the prior written consent of the copyright owner.*

Typically, a copyright holder is entitled to limit the rights that are conveyed to purchasers of the work.

Remember that the relevant sticks in the copyright bundle here are the right to reproduce the work, to create derivative works, to display the work publicly, and to distribute copies of the work to the public by sale, lease, or some other way. Since the thing that's copyrighted is the pattern, not the thing created by using the pattern, those rights are limited to the drawings and diagrams that the pattern-maker created.

So you can make the patterned items, but *you can't reproduce and sell the pattern itself*. This is a similar situation to landscape designers and gardeners: their plans are copyrightable, but the yards and gardens are not theirs.

Trying to figure out what exactly a copyright holder will allow you to do with patterns or plans can be tricky. First, look for an explicit statement of terms on the work itself (usually found on the edge of a piece of fabric; on the copyright or introduction page of a book; on any packaging; or at the bottom of a webpage). You can also contact the copyright holder or their agent directly to request permission for your use.

Be Creative in Writing Instructions

First, remember that the *idea* of what your pattern is for is not something that can be copyrighted, no matter how creative or unique it may be. So don't be alarmed when you see someone walking down the street wearing or carrying something obviously made from your pattern, because that's what your pattern is for.

At the same time, the *instructions* for using your pattern may or may not be copyrightable, depending on how uniquely-written they are; simple step-by-step instructions are unlikely to be approved for copyright; the more creative and less utilitarian the text, the more protectible it is.

So, for example, if your instructions read "cut out panel A and sew it to panel C using a French seam," you're not likely to get a copyright. On the other hand, if your instructions say "Attach panel A to panel C. I prefer to use a French seam, because it reminds me of my Grandma Clara. When she made these, she always said "I know they call this a French seam, but I think of it as a Mexican seam," and told the story about how she learned it from her neighbor when she was living in Cuernavaca in the 1940s..." this more personal, creative, idiosyncratic instruction is more likely to be worthy of copyright.

PATTERN BOOKS

Keep in mind that the drawings of the pattern are copyrightable, if they are sufficiently original,[148] and anyone who copies or distributes them is violating your copyright. Under law, you're entitled to collect your patterns in a book and sell it to people who will then make the items. They're not entitled to distribute the patterns, and you're not entitled to stop them from making items out of the patterns.

When thinking about copyrighting a pattern book, think of it this way: if you wanted to copyright a vase, you could do that, but you can't copyright the clay, the glaze, the pigments or paint used to make the vase. Similarly, the collection of patterns in a book can be copyrighted, but not individual patterns contained in it. It's a tricky business.[149]

No Clear Legal Guidance

The problem with patterns is that there's not a lot of case law to guide us. With other aspects of copyright, such as parody and fair use, there are hundreds of court cases that apply the law to specific facts, and give us precedents we can rely on in the future. Here, though, there's not much.

The bottom line is that a drawing of a jacket may be copyrighted as a creative work, but the patterns and instructions for making it, and the jacket itself once made, are considered useful articles and are not able to be copyrighted.

Some designers try to get around this inconvenient truth in various creative ways, some of which are more effective than

---

[148] *Id.*, § 920.1
[149] See, e.g., US Copyright Office, *Compendium*, Chapter 900: Jewelry, § 920.1 (rev'd 2021)

others. Slapping a © on a pattern is a lovely gesture, and may frighten off some people, but it's essentially meaningless. More effective, though, is the use of licenses. If a user has to click a box to agree to license terms in order to download a pattern from a website, or if a book states that by using its patterns the reader is agreeing to its terms, the designer can legally control how the pattern is used. For example, the designer could require that the pattern be used only for personal use and not for resale. The designer is simply leveraging the license agreement to take the place of and enforceable copyright.

PROJECT BOOKS

"A how-to book explains how to perform certain skills and techniques."[150] How-to and project books are educational, because they are designed to teach someone how to do something. But like any book of patterns or instructions, any creative content can be copyrighted: photos, drawing, diagrams, text, etc., if they are "sufficiently creative."[151] But the project that's being taught—the craft, the clothing, whatever—is an idea, and therefore not protectable by copyright.[152]

To register a pattern, stencil, or how-to book, the applicant should describe the copyrightable content in the deposit using terms such as "text, "2-D artwork," "photograph," or "technical drawing," as applicable. Applicants should not assert a claim in "pattern," "project," "activity," or "craft."—because the Copyright Office doesn't generally recognize those as copyrightable things.[153]

T-SHIRTS

These days, t-shirts are a major method of communicating. We wear t-shirts that announce our pop culture interests, our music

---

[150] *Id.*, § 920.3
[151] *Id.*
[152] 17 USC § 102(b)
[153] *Id.*, § 920.4

heroes, our political affiliation, our favorite sports team, the beverage we like best, or our unique sense of humor. When you buy a t-shirt in a store that displays a trademarked logo (think Coca-Cola or Nike), the t-shirt manufacturer has obtained (and paid for) a license from the company to reproduce their logo on a shirt. When you buy the shirt, part of what you're paying for is the cost of that license.

Of course, t-shirts are not copyrightable, since they are useful items. But the design or imprint *is* protectable, as a unique creative work.

When you're printing your own t-shirts, the same rules apply. It doesn't matter how much you love Bart Simpson; if you put his face on a t-shirt, you're violating copyright. If you put Bart's face on a shirt and wear it only when you're alone inside your house, it might be considered a fair use (analogous to making a copy of a TV show to watch later); but the minute you have friends over, or wear the shirt outside your house, you're "displaying" it "publicly" and that's infringe-worthy since public display is one of the copyright holder's bundle of sticks.

That holds true not just for characters, but for logos, designs, song lyrics, quotes from novels, restaurant names...anything that someone holds a copyright and/or trademark on. Your weakest possible defense is to claim that your shirt is honoring its subject, and providing free publicity in their support. "Free publicity" is worth every cent someone pays for it, which is to say it's not worth anything. Businesses think quite a bit about their brand and marketing, and spend a lot of money to highly-paid and experienced staff to develop marketing, advertising, and publicity strategies. Your free contribution is *not* part of their overall sales plan, and will not be welcomed warmly.

Remember, though, that there is such a thing as fair use. But if you're going to use other people's IP for parody purposes, though, just be sure that it's crystal clear what you're doing. Otherwise you may find yourself on the receiving end of an unfriendly cease-and-desist letter from the copyright holder's lawyers.

There's another bright spot: online retailers like Redbubble and TeePublic have entered into general license agreements with a variety of pop-culture copyright holders that permit designers to create t-shirt imprints without obtaining individual permissions, subject to the copyright owners' approval. On Redbubble's homepage, you can find a frequently-updated list of the content licenses available, as well as the terms of the license; copyright holders have provided specific lists of acceptable and unacceptable designs.

For instance, the producers of the "Borderlands" video game series encourage the use of original artwork in a variety of styles, not repurposed screenshots, as well as humor, designs appropriate for all ages, and ask that you "treat brand elements such as the vault symbol with respect and do not distort them."[154] On the other hand, designers are asked to avoid graphic violence, gore, blood or cursing on shirts (an ironic requirement, given the contents of the game itself). "Don't submit works that are vulgar, hyper-violent, obscene, racist, hateful, defamatory, political, or otherwise divisive or inappropriate. Works that are deemed as offensive will not be approved and taken down."[155]

Overall, your best bet is to be creative: make up your own catchy slogans, create your own imprint-worthy geometric designs, develop your own snarky cartoon cats. If you created it, you hold copyright, and you don't need anyone's permission to do anything you want with it.

---

[154] Redbubble Partner Program Guidelines, "Borderlands" at https://help.redbubble.com/hc/en-us/articles/360033358731
[155] *Id.*

So what do you take away from all this? Four simple points to remember:

1. Although copyright may not protect "useful articles" of clothing, a good alternative for clothing designers to protect their work may lie in trademark.
2. Costumes are generally considered useful articles by the Copyright Office.
3. Watch out for licensing limitations when using published patterns.
4. Many t-shirt retailers have obtained blanket licenses that allow designers to create works depicting copyrighted characters and text.

Chapter 8
Performing Arts

COMEDY

It's not news that people steal jokes. Comedians have made whole routines around the trials of other comedians stealing their jokes. And as with most things copyright-related, the Internet has made stealing jokes easier and simpler than ever before, which is frustrating for comedians who work hard to come up with material, only to see it spread across the Web moments after their set is over.

First some basics: Like anything else, comedy is only copyrightable if it's original, in a tangible form, includes creative elements, and has been published. "Published," as we've established, includes public performance, so a thirty-minute set in a basement comedy club counts. It's important to remember that only the *words* of the joke itself are protected—the way the joke is worded and told—but not the underlying *idea* of the joke. That is, no one holds a copyright on a priest, a minister, and a rabbi walking into a bar. What they do and say once they're there, though, can be protected.

The problem faced by comedians, though, is that there is a huge professional stigma attached to being seen as a "joke thief"— there's a code of honor among standup comedians that they simply don't steal one another's material (even when they occasionally do). The Internet, and specifically joke aggregation sites, have made it difficult for comedians to protect their routines. Once a joke is uploaded without attribution to a website and freely discoverable by others, liked on social media, made into memes, and generally spread around everywhere, the comic who wrote it often has to abandon it, because they don't want to look like they've stolen it from online—even though they wrote it in the first place!

For example, comedy writer Alex Kaseberg posted several jokes on Twitter between December 2014 and February 2015. In multiple cases, identical or nearly-identical jokes were told within days of the posts by Conan O'Brien on his late-night talk show. In 2017, Kaseberg sued, citing five jokes allegedly stolen by O'Brien. The court denied O'Brien's motion to throw out the lawsuit, finding a sufficient basis for trial on at least some of the jokes in question. However, the $600,000 lawsuit was settled out of court before trial.[156] O'Brien, however, went to great pains to explain the case and emphasize his innocence, writing in a 2019 op-ed in *Variety*, "Short of murder, stealing material is the worst thing any comic can be accused of..."[157]

The challenges posed by social media cause a lot of comedians to not post jokes from their stand-up routines on blogs, websites, Twitter, Instagram, and Facebook at all. Instead, they create jokes solely for the purpose of promoting themselves on social media, and keep their stand-up jokes safely off the Web.[158] Since the general public doesn't share the comedians' ethical

---

[156] *Kaseberg v. Conaco*, 260 F. Supp. 3d 1229 (S.D. Cal. 2017).
[157] Conan O'Brien, "Why I Decided to Settle a Lawsuit Over Alleged Joke Stealing," Variety (May 9, 2019)
https://variety.com/2019/biz/news/conan-obrien-jokes-lawsuit-alex-kaseberg-settlement-1203210214/
[158] Hannah Pham, "Standing Up for Stand-Up Comedy: Joke Theft and the Relevance of Copyright Law and
Social Norms in the Social Media Age," 30 Fordham Intell. Prop. Media & Ent. L.J. 55 (2019). https://ir.lawnet.fordham.edu/iplj/vol30/iss1/2

concerns about joke originality, the social media posts spread rapidly. Unfortunately, nothing stops audience members from posting their favorite jokes from a stand-up set on their social media platforms, transcribed or in video form, or sharing them with joke aggregator sites. And as was mentioned earlier, once a joke is roaming free on the Web, the comedian generally has to abandon it or be accused of plagiarizing their own material.

The Comedy Cellar in New York prohibits photography and audio/video recording during live shows. To ensure compliance with the policy, the venue requires audience members to seal their phones in disposable bags until the show is over. The goal is to prevent joke theft as well as the posting of out-of-context or off-the-cuff content that could reflect badly on the comedian.[159]

So what does all this mean? It means that for a comedian, being the victim of copyright infringement is a constant threat. Under law, jokes are entitled to only "thin" copyright protection—that means, the infringing joke has to be virtually identical in words and structure to the original.[160] That's sometimes a tough thing to prove. Also, copyright infringement lawsuits can be expensive and time-consuming, and in a profession where both time and cash can sometimes be in short supply, that makes defending one's jokes a challenge. The best bet is probably what comedians are already doing: keep your best material for live performances and recordings, and just remember that any material you post on social media will be unusable the moment you post it.

---

[159] Hannah Pham, *supra*.

[160] See, e.g., Kaseberg v. Conaco: "Each joke begins with a factual sentence and then ... concludes with another sentence providing humorous commentary on the preceding facts. Facts, of course, are not protected by copyright. ... And although the punchlines of the jokes are creative, they are nonetheless constrained by the limited number of variations that would [be] humorous ... This merits only thin protection. The standard for infringement must therefore also be some form of 'virtual identity.'"

Case Study

In the Broadway play, *Hand to God*,[161] a boy and his hand puppet develop distinct, conflicting personalities.[162] To illustrate this, the playwright has the boy, Jason, perform part of Abbott and Costello's famous "Who's on First?" routine with the puppet, Tyrone. When the girl Jason is trying to impress asks him if he wrote the routine, Jason lies and says yes, he did. Tyrone calls him on his lie, and that's how the play establishes that the two are becoming separate personalities. The heirs of Abbott and Costello sued, claiming copyright infringement. The playwright argued that the use was fair, because it was transformative. The court rejected both sides' claims, ultimately finding that the use was not fair, but that the comics' estates had failed to establish that they held copyright.[163] The court explained:

> Far from altering Who's on First? To the point where it is "barely recognizable" within the Play...defendants' use appears not to have altered the Routine at all. The Play may convey a dark critique of society, but it does not transform Abbott and Costello's Routine so that it conveys that message. To the contrary, it appears that the Play specifically has its characters perform Who's on First? without alteration so that the audience will readily recognize both the famous Routine and the boy's false claim to having created it. ...Defendants nevertheless maintain that using the Routine for such a "dramatic," rather than comedic, purpose was transformative. The argument will not bear close scrutiny. ... To advance the plot of the Play—specifically, to have the puppet Tyrone take on a persona distinct from that of Jason—defendants needed Jason to lie about something and for Tyrone to call him on it. But the

---

[161] By Robert Askins; performed off-Broadway 2011-2014; and on Broadway at the Booth Theatre 2015-2016.
[162] *TCA Television Corp. v. McCollum*, No. 16-134 (2d Cir. 2016)
[163] The routine had gone through a number of versions, licenses, and transfers between 1940 and 2016, making it unclear who—if anyone—actually held copyright any more.

particular subject of the lie, the Routine, appears irrelevant to that purpose.[164]

That is, whatever his intent may have been, the playwright had simply plopped the comedians' routine into his play without altering its published words or how it was performed, and that was not transformative.

DANCE

So you like to dance? There's good news, bad news, and more good news. The good news is you're free to dance like no one's watching. The bad news is that movements or dance steps alone are not copyrightable. That means the basic steps of the waltz, the hustle, the most recent viral TikTok dance, the first position in classical ballet, social dances (like square or line dancing) or simple movements (what you do in your living room when no one's looking) are not copyrightable, even if you've added your own unique twist to them.[165] But the other good news is that *choreography* is copyrightable, if it meets the law's requirements for complexity that distinguish it from "mere dance."

Choreography

Works of choreography are specifically protectable by copyright.[166] As stated earlier, though, performances of dance works and choreography aren't protectable unless they're made tangible through video or choreographic notation. Typically, choreography works include such elements as

- Rhythmic movement in a defined space
- Compositional arrangement

---

[164] *TCA Television Corp. v. McCollum*, No. 16-134 (2d Cir. 2016)
[165] US Copyright Office, *Compendium*, Chapter 8900: Performing Art Works, § 805.5
[166] 17 USC § 102(a)(4)

- Musical or textual accompaniment (that provides a rhythm or theme for the work)
- Dramatic content (with or without a story)
- Created by a human author for presentation to a human audience by skilled human performers[167]

These elements distinguish artistic works of choreography from "mere" dance. Dance, according to the copyright law, is basically something people do by themselves for their own amusement. Choreography is done as a performance by skilled performers.

One way choreographic works are protected is if they're recorded somehow in choreographic notation, for instance, or video.

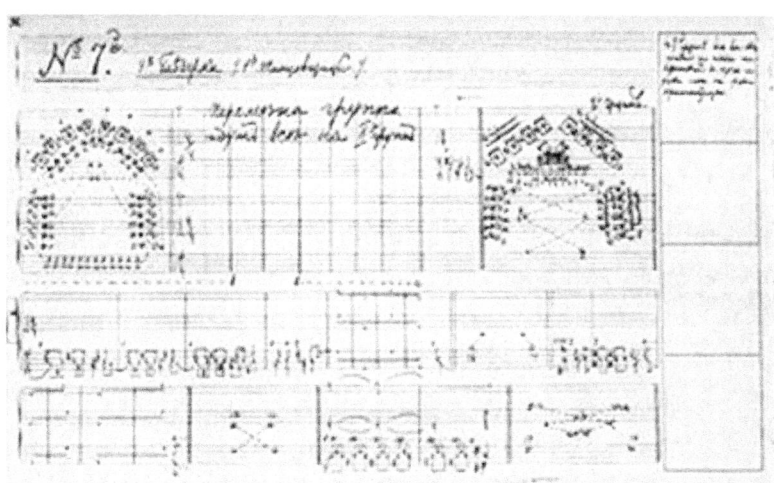

Bayadere-Stepanov Choreographic Notation, circa 1900. [Source: Wikimedia Commons. Public domain image]

It seems simple, but of course there are exceptions. Common movements or activities, like yoga positions, line dances and exercise routines, are not copyrightable, even when they are

---

[167] US Copyright Office, *Compendium*, Chapter 8900: Performing Art Works, § 805.2

unique. Individual ballet or dance positions that are commonly used are also not copyrightable.

> *A choreographic work "represents a related series of dance movements and patterns" organized into an integrated, coherent, and expressive compositional whole. Simple dance steps or ordinary movements are not copyrightable.*[168]

PERFORMANCE ART

Copyright law clearly protects the *performing* arts (generally defined as musical works, including any accompanying words; sound recordings; dramatic works, including any accompanying music; choreographic works; pantomimes; audiovisual works; and motion pictures, prepared for the purpose of being performed directly before an audience or indirectly by means of a device or process.[169] We look at those elements elsewhere, but for this topic it's pretty clear what's missing: the unique niche of *performance* art.

"Performance art" is a whole different ballgame. Performance art is "a genre in which the actions by the artist are the final, actual piece of art":

> [The] art is presented "live," usually by the artist but sometimes with collaborators or performers. ... The foremost purpose of performance art has almost always been to challenge the conventions of traditional forms of visual art such as painting and sculpture. ... Performance art borrows styles and ideas from other forms of art, or sometimes from other forms of activity not associated

---

[168] *Horgan v. MacMillan Inc.*, 789 F.2d 157 (1986) (quoting *Compendium* (2d) § 450.03(a)).

[169] US Copyright Office, *Compendium*, Chapter 800: Glossary, citing 37 CFR § 202.3(b)(1)(ii).

with art, like ritual, or work-like tasks, ... dance, and even sport."[170]

In other words, performance art is an expressive art form in which the artist is the creator, the subject, and the canvass. And that's where the copyright question becomes a little thorny.

Remember that copyright protections apply to works that are "fixed in a tangible medium of expression."[171] The very nature of performance art is to be live, spontaneous, interactive, responsive, contextual—things that are pretty much the opposite of "fixed in a tangible medium of expression."

For example, Marina Abramović is one of the most famous modern performance artists. She has performed at both the Guggenheim and the Museum of Modern Art in New York. One of her pieces is called "The Artist is Present," and involves Abramović seated at a table, while museum attendees are invited to sit and stare at her while she stares back. It is a wholly interactive work, with no time limits outside MoMA's operating hours.[172] Another notable example of performance art is Yoko Ono's "Cut Piece," in which "Ono sat silent upon a stage as viewers walked up to her and cut away her clothing with a pair of scissors. This forced people to take responsibility for their voyeurism and to reflect upon how even passive witnessing could potentially harm the subject of perception."[173] Then there's Chris Burden's 1971 performance art piece, "Shoot," in which "Burden stood in front of a wall while one friend shot him in the arm with a .22 long rifle... in front of a small, private

---

[170] The Art Story Foundation, "Performance Art" at https://www.theartstory.org/movement/performance-art/
[171] 17 USC §101
[172] Henry Lydiate and Daniel McClean, "Performance Art and the Law," https://www.artquest.org.uk/artlaw-article/performance-art-and-the-law-2/ (2011)
[173] Anne Marie Butler, "Performance Art Movement Overview and Analysis", TheArtStory.org [https://www.theartstory.org/movement/performance-art/] (2019)

audience."[174] And finally, performance artist Millie Brown is well-known for vomiting green soy milk onto Lady Gaga while the singer was performing at SXSW in 2014.[175]

Keep in mind, though, that performance art pieces are often highly conceptual—that is, they're about ideas, and ideas are not copyrightable. What's more, once a performance art piece happens, it's gone, which is sort of the whole point.

But performance artists are not completely without the ability to protect their work through copyright. Remember that while dance performances aren't copyrightable, their underlying choreographic notes *are*. The same holds true here: while a spontaneous live performance may not be copyrightable, the "script" for the performance is, as would be a video or photographs of the performance.

So if you're creating a performance piece, commit as much detail as possible to a written script or choreography plan. While performance art doesn't fall neatly into the copyright law's categories of protected content, it is arguable a "dramatic work," which is fully copyrightable. If the performance piece has a script and formal choreography, it's more similar to a traditional dramatic work and so more likely to be copyrightable.

THEATER

The US Copyright Office defines five types of "dramatic works:"[176]

- *Stage Plays*—a script prepared for production in a theater, on a stage, for a live audience.

---

[174] *Id.*

[175] Diane Tsai, "Artist Who Puked on Lady Gaga at SXSW Defends Her Craft," time.com, https://time.com/30105/ video-artist-who-puked-on-lady-gaga-at-sxsw-defends-her-craft/ (March 19, 2014)

[176] US Copyright Office, *Compendium*, Chapter 800: Works of the Performing Arts, § 804 (rev'd 2021)

- *Musical Plays*—a work in which musical and dramatic material are both integral parts of the dramatic work, such as musicals, operas, and operettas.
- *Screenplays*—a script prepared for production in a motion picture.
- *Teleplays*—a script prepared for streaming or broadcast on television.
- *Radio Plays*—a script prepared for broadcast on radio or via streaming media, such as podcasts or other audio-only platforms.

The elements of a typical dramatic work include plot, characters, dialog, stage directions, blocking, musical references or notation, and sketches of sets or costumes.[177]

Like any other written work, theatrical works are certainly copyrightable, if they are made up of original material, in a tangible form, and performed publicly. The copyright holder (presumably the playwright) holds all the sticks in the copyright bundle like any other author, and it's up to them whether or not to let others stage productions of their theatrical work.

All the principles of copyright law apply to plays and musicals, including public domain[178]. No permissions are needed to perform Shakespeare's Macbeth *or Oscar Wilde's* The Importance of Being Earnest, *for instance (unless you're using abridged or edited versions, because the editor or abridger will hold copyright over that specific production). Similarly, Ibsen's* Hedda Gabler *and August Strindberg's* Miss Julie *are also public domain—but unless you're performing them in the original Swedish or Norwegian, you'll need permission of the author of the English translation—unless that, too, has fallen into the public domain.[179]*

---

[177] *Id.*
[178] See Chapter 1
[179] US Copyright Office, *Circular 14: Copyright in Derivative Works and Compilations* (rev'd 2020)

It is infringement to perform any copyrighted work without a license from the copyright holder. It doesn't matter if it's a full production or a reading; a professional, semi-professional, or amateur production; or whether it's in a commercial theatre, a public park, or a school auditorium. Failure to obtain a performance license can result in an expensive lawsuit, because copyright holders are entitled to protect their work.

Most playwrights use a permissions clearing house, rather than deal with performance requests themselves. For instance, playwrights can use Music Theater International (MTI), Concord Theatricals, Broadway Play Publishing, Dramatist's Play Service, or Playscripts. There are numerous other licensing agencies as well. Basically, the performance rights organizations (PROs) represent the playwright as an agent, and take a percentage of the licensing fee as compensation.

Ⓒase Study Theaterpalooza is an organization that runs youth musical theater lessons in Virginia and Maryland. The final project of the class is the production and performance of a musical. The students pay tuition, and the performances are open to the ticket-buying public. Between 2015 and 2018, Theaterpalooza presented student performances of *Mary Poppins*, *Annie*, *Mama Mia!*, and *Hairspray*,[180] all without obtaining a license from MTI. MTI sued, and Theaterpalooza did not respond, resulting in a default judgment for MTI of $450,000 plus attorney's fees, and a permanent injunction against Theaterpalooza mounting any further unlicensed productions. Despite Theaterpalooza's positive efforts to introduce young people to musical theater, and their argument that the whole thing was a simple billing issue (and that many of their productions were original), performing copyrighted works without a license in place is never a good idea.[181]

---

[181] MTI Enterprises. Inc. v. Theaterpalooza Cmty. Theater Prods., Inc., Case No. 1:18-cv-650 (TSE/IDD) (E.D. Va. Dec. 7, 2018)

Even with a license, the permission to perform a copyrighted play or musical is permission to only perform the work as written. While a director can always give a production their own individual spin, a license does not include the ability to cut, edit, or add to the copyrighted work. When a theatre in San Francisco cut Stephen Adly Guirgis's play, *The Last Days of Judas Iscariot*, from two hours to 80 minutes (so that two shows a night could be performed) and eliminated characters due to budget constraints, the playwright first sent a cease-and-desist letter insisting the production be shut down. Guirgis ultimately allowed the performance as long as a disclaimer was included in the program stating that "The play you are seeing tonight has been improperly and extensively cut & edited. These edits were made without permission, against the wishes of the playwright, and in violation of Federal Copyright Law."[182]

Off-Script: Other Theatrical Designs & Concepts

Stage directions, annotations, prop lists, blocking, sketches of set designs, and floor plans are usually not included in scripts available for licensing. That's because those elements are not usually the copyrighted property of the playwright. But whose property are they? That's a tricky question.

The US Copyright Office says "Illustrations of costumes, scenery, sets, props, and lighting may be included in a dramatic work. If the illustrations are copyrightable, they may be registered as visual arts works. A textual description of such works may also be registered as a literary work, **but the registration does not extend to the costume, prop, set or lighting itself**.[183]

---

[182] Julie Musbach, "Update: Shelton Theatre's Unsanctioned Adaptation is Shut Down Due to Copyright Infringement," Broadway World (August 6, 2017) https://www.broadwayworld.com/article/UPDATE-Shelton-Theatres-Unsanctioned-Adaptation-is-Shut-Down-Due-to-Copyright-Infringement-20170806

[183] US Copyright Office, *Compendium:* Works of the Performing Arts, § 804.3(F) (rev'd 2021)

Copyright only protects works that are "fixed in a tangible medium," so the actual set of a theatre production isn't copyrightable, because while it is tangible, it is, by its nature, impermanent and not fixed in any medium. A set designer can—and often does—create sketches and models of set designs, and these can be copyrighted as visual works. Costumes are also tricky.[184] Because clothing is a "useful article," a play's costumes are probably not copyrightable, although sketches and patterns may be.

This is what copyright law says about other non-script elements of a theatrical production:

Plot: Not copyrightable, because an idea can't be copyrighted.[185]

Characters: Copyright law does not protect the name or the general idea for a character.[186]

Stage Directions, Blocking, and Stage Business: Instructions for how actors are to move or behave on stage are not copyrightable "because [they represent] common body movements which are not subject to copyright protection."[187]

Music: Original musical compositions included in a theatrical work *are* copyrightable.[188]

If a production wants to mimic the original Broadway version of a play, for instance, the best practice is to contact the original director, set and costume designers for permission to reproduce their work. An even better option is for the production to come up with its own original vision.

---

[184] See Chapter 4
[185] US Copyright Office, *Compendium:* Works of the Performing Arts, § 804.3(A) (rev'd 2021)
[186] *Id.* at § 804.3(B)
[187] *Id.* at §§804.3(D),(D)(1), and (D)(2)
[188] *Id.* at §804.3(E)

School Productions

There is no educational use exemption for performing copyrighted plays and musicals in a school setting without a license. A theater's status as nonprofit or educational is irrelevant to the need to obtain a license from the copyright holder—although some PROs may offer lower license fees for school productions.

A standard performance license does not include permission to alter dialogue or lyrics for any reason, including production time or to remove potentially inappropriate language or concepts. If your high school theater department wants to perform Cabaret *or* Avenue Q *in the auditorium, be prepared to deal with the strong adult themes and profanity in both works. Some copyright holders have allowed "school versions" of their plays to be created that eliminate or soften adult themes and language in dialogue and lyrics.*

 **So what do you take away from all this? Four simple points to remember:**

1. While dances can't be copyrighted, choreography published in a fixed medium can be.
2. Jokes are absolutely copyrightable.
3. Be careful when performing public domain works that you're not using a protected translation or adaptation.
4. School productions are not exempt from copyright, although school versions of scripts and reduced licensing fees may be available.

Chapter 9
Social Media

COPYRIGHT, LICENSES, AND SOCIAL MEDIA

The biggest challenge with posting content on social media platforms is that while your content is still protected by copyright, it's phenomenally easy for people to copy, share, and even create derivative works from what you've posted. And generally, because they haven't read this book, they're doing it thinking that because content is freely available on the Internet, it is automatically free for them to use. We know they're wrong, but they don't, so they do it all the time.

The other major risk to creators using social media is that they will inadvertently violate someone else's copyright.

When you walk into a store and they're playing current pop hits, they've subscribed to a service that pays a license fee to the record companies (and some pennies go to the artists, too). If someone posts a video of scenes from their hiking trip on YouTube or TikTok and uses the song "Bad Romance" as the background music, they're basically broadcasting the song (that is, "distributing" in copyright terms) without Lady Gaga or Interscope's permission. The Recording Industry of America (RIA) polices in-store music and issues fines to stores that play unlicensed music. YouTube, TikTok, and other platforms are trying to avoid being sued for illegal broadcast—companies hate being sued because it looks bad and costs money. Their copyright policies are to protect themselves, not to protect artists or punish content creators.

It must be said that the risk to the social media platforms of being sued is not huge. Under the Digital Millennium Copyright Act (DMCA), service providers are sheltered from liability for displaying content that infringes someone's copyright *if*:

1. the material was posted on the site by someone other than the service provider;
2. the process of posting and displaying the content is done automatically, without the service provider's direct control;
3. the service provider does not distribute the content to anyone except as an automatic response to their request;
4. the service provider doesn't keep copies of content in a publicly-accessible archive; and
5. the content is not modified by the site.[189]

The "safe shelter" offered by DMCA to online sites also requires that the sites have specific policies and procedures for dealing with copyright infringement, and that once they have received notice of an alleged infringement they act quickly to block or remove the content.[190] That's why you'll find that not only do most social media sites have detailed processes for reporting alleged infringing content, but that they generally remove or block that content quickly once they're received notice, before investigating the truth of the charge.

Be careful to be sure that your copyright is being infringed before reporting it to a social media site. Under DMCA, the intentional filing of a false claim of infringement (or falsely claiming in an appeal that your content's removal was a mistake) will leave you

---

[189] 17 USC § 512 - Limitations on liability relating to material online
[190] *Id.*

liable for any damages incurred by the other party and the social media company.[191] *If attorney's fees are involved, or if the content generated ad revenue that's been lost due to a false claim, those damages can be costly.*

If you frequent YouTube or TikTok, you've undoubtedly heard creators complaining about what they often view as copyright harassment by the platforms. But while their reading of copyright law may be extremely broad, the platforms are only trying to protect themselves against costly lawsuits—even at the expense of arguably fair uses of copyrighted content by creators.

Let's take a quick look at some copyright policies, procedures, and concerns for some major social media sites. They all comply with the DMCA, so you'll see a good bit of similarity in their processes related to infringement. Most of the policies discussed below are from the platforms' End User License Agreements (EULAs) and Terms of Service (TOS).

FACEBOOK

Facebook's copyright policy[192] is both clear and double-edged, simultaneously embracing intellectual property rights and serving as a warning against infringement: "Facebook takes intellectual property rights seriously and believes they are important to promoting expression, creativity, and innovation in our community. You own all of the content and information you post on Facebook, and you control how it is shared through your privacy and application settings. However, before sharing content on Facebook, please be sure you have the right to do so.

---

[191] *Id.* at paragraph (f)
[192] In 2021, corporate Facebook's parent corporation changed its name to Meta. "Facebook" is still the platform name.

We ask that you respect other people's copyrights, trademarks and other legal rights."[193]

Facebook provides a variety of tools to combat infringement. For instance, through its Rights Manager platform you can

- block an infringing video;
- claim any earnings from a post containing infringing content that's supported by ad revenue;
- apply a banner directly on the infringing post linking it to your content; and
- formally report the infringement to Facebook.

Facebook provides an online form for reporting copyright infringement as well.[194] If you report an infringement of your copyright, the person alleged to have infringed will receive the report number, your name and email address, details of the report, and instructions on how to appeal.[195] Anyone accused of copyright infringement can appeal to Facebook using online tools as well.[196]

License Alert!

Facebook/Meta acknowledges that you own the intellectual property rights (copyright or trademark) in content you share on the platform. However, use of the platform includes granting Facebook/Meta "a non-exclusive, transferable, sub-licensable, royalty-free, and worldwide license to host, use, distribute, modify, run, copy, publicly perform or display, translate, and

---

[193] Facebook Transparency Center, https://transparency.fb.com/policies/community-standards/intellectual-property/
[194] The form is available here: https://www.facebook.com/help/contact/1758255661104383
[195] https://www.facebook.com/help/400287850027717
[196] Https://m.facebook.com/help/contact/1653629651334864#:~:text=Use%20this%20form%20if%20something,the%20issue%20with%20them%20directly.

create derivative works of your content."[197] That means that the photo you post of you and your friends toasting the new year can be independently stored, copied, and shared by Facebook. You also automatically give Facebook/Meta permission to share your name, profile picture and history with advertisers or your friends, in order to more effectively target advertising they may be interested in. For instance, Facebook/Meta can tell your friends that you were interested in a particular product or liked an advertiser's page. The license ends when you delete your account.[198]

There's a lot of ridiculous stuff posted on Facebook to be sure, but one of the biggest examples is the "Copyright Disclaimer" hoax that circulated around social media and chain emails between 2014 and 2017, and that still rears its ugly head from time to time, because the Internet is forever. You've probably seen it:

> *I hereby declare that my copyright is attached to all of my personal details, illustrations, comics, paintings, photos and videos, etc. (as a result of the Berne Convention). For commercial use of the above my written consent is needed at all times! ... By the present communiqué, I notify Facebook that it is strictly forbidden to disclose, copy, distribute, disseminate, or take any other action against me on the basis of this profile and/or its contents...*

The thing is, of course, all of that is nonsense. For one thing, your copyright already is attached to anything you post; Facebook isn't "taking" your copyright. The only way to insulate your content from being used by Facebook under its terms of service is to delete all your content your Facebook page, contact anyone who's ever shared or reposted your content and ask them to delete it, and cancel your Facebook account. Those actions, under Facebook's terms of service, will absolutely end their

---

[197] https://www.facebook.com/terms.php
[198] *Id.*

license to use your content. Posting legal-sounding hogwash on Facebook is a waste of your time.

> *If Facebook (or Twitter, or Instagram, or any other social media platform) removes something you posted, citing their policies against offensive, misleading, or otherwise unacceptable content, their action is NOT a violation of your First Amendment right to free speech. The First Amendment prohibits the government from limiting your free speech; it doesn't apply to privately-owned platforms, even if they're publicly-traded.*

INSTAGRAM

Instagram's copyright policy is clear: "you can only post content to Instagram that doesn't violate someone else's intellectual property rights. The best way to help make sure that what you post to Instagram doesn't violate copyright law is to only post content that you've created yourself."[199]

Instagram will remove content alleged to be infringing. Like other social media sites, Instagram has an online form for reporting copyright violations.[200] That form includes the following information (all of which will be shared with the alleged infringer):[201]

- Your name, mailing address and phone number;
- A description of the infringing content;
- Information reasonably sufficient to permit Instagram to locate the infringement;
- A declaration that includes:

---

[199] Instagram Help Center, "Copyright" https://help.instagram.com/126382350847838
[200] The form is found here: https://help.instagram.com/contact/552695131608132
[201] Instagram Help Center, "Reporting Copyright Infringements" https://help.instagram.com/454951664593304

- o Your good faith belief that use of the copyrighted content is not authorized by the copyright owner or the law (i.e., not covered by fair use);
- o A statement that the information you're providing is accurate;
- o You swear or affirm that you are the owner of a copyright that is being infringed; and
- Your electronic or physical signature.

If you're accused of violating someone else's copyright on Instagram, the company encourages you to file an appeal under the Digital Millennium Copyright Act (DMCA).

License Alert!

Instagram acknowledges your copyright in your content, and doesn't claim ownership of your content. However, by using the platform you grant Instagram "a non-exclusive, royalty-free, transferable, sub-licensable, worldwide license to host, use, distribute, modify, run, copy, publicly perform or display, translate, and create derivative works of your content."[202] The license ends when you delete your content or your account.

ONLYFANS

While OnlyFans is often associated with subscription-based NSFW ("not safe for work") or adult content, a growing number of celebrities, influencers, and other content creators are using the platform to promote their projects. Because the platform enables direct interaction between content creators and their audience, it's useful in creating and maintaining fan communities. AMA ("ask me anything") features are common among both mainstream and adult-oriented OnlyFans creators.

There's also a financial appeal. Unlike YouTube or TikTok, for instance, where creators can generate ad and creator-fund

---

[202] Instagram Help Center, Terms of Use https://help.instagram.com/581066165581870

revenue at a rate of pennies-per-thousand-views,[203] OnlyFans allows creators to set subscription rates, and then takes a 20% commission, so earnings are in the creator's control and can add up quickly.[204]

A particular risk for OnlyFans creators is that users may download your content and share it on content aggregation platforms, where views don't generate revenue for you, but may be generating revenue for the other platforms. Because the OnlyFans site permits downloads, and there's no way to prevent screen recording, this presents a dilemma for OF creators. Be aware of your rights as a copyright holder, however, and don't be afraid to contact sites to demand your content be taken down. Most aggregation sites have a process for such demands and don't want to be sued for copyright infringement. Usually a polite email informing the site of the offending content, and clearly stating that you are the copyright holder, will work just fine.

License Alert!

You should be aware that by agreeing to use the OnlyFans platform, you are granting the company a license to use your copyrighted content "to perform any act restricted by any intellectual property right (including copyright)"[205] reproduce, make available and communicate to the public, display, perform, distribute, translate, and create adaptations or derivative works of your Content, and otherwise deal in your Content. in a way that's "perpetual, non-exclusive, worldwide, royalty-free, sublicensable, assignable and transferable by [OnlyFans]."[206]

---

[203] TikTok's revenue sharing plan pays 2 to 4 cents per 1000 views, for example.
[204] https://blog.onlyfans.com/how-to-make-your-content-pay-keep-the-subscribers-coming/
[205] OnlyFans Terms of Service 10(b) https://onlyfans.com/terms.html
[206] OnlyFans Terms of Service 10(c) https://onlyfans.com/terms.html

That means that you're giving OnlyFans a free, never-ending license to add watermarks, text, and stickers to your posts that will continue even if you leave the platform, and that they can transfer your license to someone else if they want to. OnlyFans promises not to try to sell your content, but they have the right to transfer it to another company in the event of a sale or merger.

As with any other platform, you can't use copyrighted music on OnlyFans. Creators on OnlyFans generally use public domain or licensed music, to avoid infringement. If you're filming in a public space and there's music playing, you'll need a license or the ability to edit it out.

TIKTOK

TikTok has a clear and direct copyright policy: "TikTok respects the intellectual property rights of others, and we expect you to do the same. TikTok's Terms of Service and Community Guidelines do not allow posting, sharing, or sending any content that violates or infringes someone else's copyrights, trademarks or other intellectual property rights."[207]

Remember that you own the copyright in original video content you post. TikTok offers a variety of music you can use as well, all of which is under license from the original artists. When you allow others to "stitch" with your video, you're giving them permission to create a transformative work—their own, original video—that comments on, parodies, or reinforces the message of your own video. If you don't want other people using your videos, don't select Allow Stitch. On the other hand, if your video is public anyone can record your sound and use it themselves. This is particularly problematic for some comedians, who often find their skits or jokes being lip-synched by other TikTokkers without attribution. That's a violation of their copyright. Similarly, using copyrighted music outside of TikTok's license structure and without permission, is

---

[207] https://www.tiktok.com/legal/copyright-policy

technically a violation of the original artist's copyright, and will result in your video being taken down by TikTok. (As mentioned in the chapter on Music, however, your own original cover version of copyrighted music may be permitted.)

TikTok provides an online Copyright Infringement Report to request the removal of alleged infringing content, and the content in question will be suppressed pending investigation. The accused will be provided with your contact information, including your name, email address and details of the complaint.[208] The accused can file a Counter-Notification Form if they believe they have a fair use or other defense.[209]

A finding of copyright infringement will result in permanent full or partial removal of the offending content. (For instance, infringing music may be muted from a video, or the entire video may be removed.) Repeated or flagrant infringements will result in a temporary or permanent ban from the platform.

License Alert!

As with other platforms, your use of TikTok *automatically* grants the company an "unconditional irrevocable, non-exclusive, royalty-free, fully transferable, perpetual worldwide license"[210] to use most of the sticks in your bundle of rights. While the company fully acknowledges that you still own your own copyright, your use of the platform grants TikTok the rights

> *to use, modify, adapt, reproduce, make derivative works of, publish and/or transmit, and/or distribute and to authorize other users of the Services and other third-parties to view, access, use, download, modify, adapt, reproduce, make derivative works of, publish and/or*

---

[208] https://www.tiktok.com/legal/report/Copyright
[209] https://www.tiktok.com/legal/report/counternotification.
[210] TikTok Terms of Service, "User-Generated Content" https://www.tiktok.com/legal/terms-of-service

> *transmit your User Content in any format and on any platform....*[211]

TWITTER

Twitter's copyright statement is direct: "Twitter respects the intellectual property rights of others and expects users of the Services to do the same. We will respond to notices of alleged copyright infringement that comply with applicable law and are properly provided to us."[212]

If someone infringes your copyright by using your content without permission, you'll need to provide Twitter with:

- Identification of the infringed copyrighted work;
- Identification of the content or activity that is claimed to be infringing that you wish to have removed;
- Information (such as a URL, link, or screen capture that's reasonably sufficient for Twitter to locate the content in question;
- Your contact information (address, telephone number, and email);
- A statement that you have a good faith belief that use of the content is not authorized by the copyright owner;
- A sworn statement that the information you're providing in the notification is accurate; and
- Your physical or electronic signature.[213]

Twitter can remove content alleged to be infringing, and will terminate a user's account if they are a repeat infringer.[214]

---

[211] *Id.*
[212] Twitter User Agreement, 9. Copyright Policy
[213] *Id.*
[214] *Id.*

License Alert!

Like other platforms, your use of Twitter grants the company a "worldwide, non-exclusive, royalty-free license (with the right to sublicense) to use, copy, reproduce, process, adapt, modify, publish, transmit, display and distribute"[215] your content. You may notice that the rights listed there are basically *all* the sticks in your bundle, including the rights to transform and translate your content.[216]

The license is needed by Twitter so that they can publish, display, and distribute your content worldwide on their platform, which is why you're tweeting so it's probably OK with you. What's interesting, though, is that the Twitter license also gives them the right to "provide, promote, and improve the Services and to make [your content] available to other companies, organizations or individuals for … syndication, broadcast, distribution, Retweet, promotion or publication."[217]

Twitter's terms make clear, too, that you are not entitled to any payment for any of the licenses you're granting or the activities they may do with your content, stating that your right to use Twitter is sufficient compensation for the rights you're granting the platform.

YOUTUBE

"Creators should only upload videos that they have made or that they're authorized to use. That means they should not upload videos they didn't make, or use content in their videos that someone else owns the copyright to, such as music tracks,

---

[215] Twitter Terms of Service, 3. Content on the Services https://twitter.com/en/tos
[216] *Id.*
[217] *Id.*

snippets of copyrighted programs, or videos made by other users, without necessary authorizations."[218]

YouTube has an online system for reporting copyright infringement and submitting a request to have the infringing content taken down.[219] If the accused infringer convinces you the use is a fair one, you can retract your report.[220] A successful takedown request will result in a "strike" against the infringer, whose account will be suspended for a week, and be required to complete copyright education coursework provided by YouTube.[221] Three copyright strikes will result in account termination, removal of all videos, and being prohibited from creating new channels.

> *It's commonly believed that there's a "30 second rule" that allows the use of the first 30 seconds of a song, but like most common beliefs about copyright, that's not true in either copyright law or YouTube policy. YouTube is clear that any use of copyrighted content is wrong, but a relatively new policy permits single-digit snippets of music (less than ten seconds) and "incidental music"—for instance, a video made in a coffee shop where there's music playing, or outdoors and a passing car is playing recognizable music. Copyright policies won't be strictly enforced against content creators under those circumstances.*[222]

---

[218] https://www.youtube.com/howyoutubeworks/policies/copyright/

[219] https://studio.youtube.com/channel/UCyVVMuGE9IDEy8WVEe7NtlA/copyright/history

[220] https://support.google.com/youtube/answer/2807691?hl=en#:~:text=Unless%20the%20uploader%20already%20deleted,restore%20the%20content%20to%20YouTube.&text=If%20you%20submitted%20a%20takedown%20request%20in%20error%2C%20you%20can,to%20copyright%40youtube.com.&text=Note%3A%20We%20can%20only%20accept%20a%20retraction%20of%20the%20takedown%20request.

[221] https://support.google.com/youtube/answer/2802032. Two strikes will result in a two-week suspension.

[222] https://support.google.com/youtube/thread/12069598

License Alert!

By using the YouTube platform, you are automatically granting YouTube "a worldwide, non-exclusive, royalty-free, sublicensable and transferable license to use that Content (including to reproduce, distribute, prepare derivative works, display and perform it) in connection with [YouTube's] business..."[223] You also grant them the right to monetize your content.[224]

In addition, you're granting all YouTube users the right to view your content, but YouTube is clear that the license is strictly to allow your content to be displayed and "performed" on the platform at the user's demand. Since you're presumably posting videos on YouTube so that people will see them, this makes sense. However, you are not granting any license or permission for users to do anything with your content outside of YouTube.

Unlike some platforms, when you remove your content or delete your account, YouTube's license will expire after "a commercially reasonable period of time"[225]—although they reserve the right to archive (but not display) copies of your videos on their servers indefinitely.

If you're posting reviews or reaction videos on YouTube, you pretty much have to include at least some of the song or movie or TV show or game you're reviewing. Here are a few simple things you can do—in addition to crediting the artists and production companies—to lessen the likelihood of a strike:

1. Keep your use of any copyrighted content short. The shorter the better.
2. If you must play a full song or video, break it up into short pieces and leave some pieces out, so it's clearly not the full piece.

---

[223] *Id.*
[224] *Id.*
[225] *Id.*

3. Distort audio clips: run a song at a higher speed or leave muted gaps.
4. Distort video clips: insert digital stickers, distorting filters, or your own semi-transparent logo on video clips. Simply flipping an image is usually not sufficient.
5. Make sure you're always visible in the video, preferably overlapping the images you're using, but clearly interacting with them.

None of these steps necessarily guarantees that YouTube's automated and human watchdogs won't slap you down, but they may help.

 **So what do you take away from all this? Four simple points to remember:**

1. All social media platforms have some sort of licensing in place in exchange for posting content on them. Be aware of the license terms, but don't be too worried about it.
2. If you include other people's copyrighted content in your social media posts, you are infringing their copyright, and the platform may have to remove your content to protect itself from lawsuits. To help prevent take-downs, use as little unlicensed content as possible. If you're doing reviews or reactions, use snippets, and distort audio and video content.
3. There is no "30 second rule" that lets you legally infringe others' copyrights if you just infringe a little bit.
4. If you suspect your content is being infringed, be certain before you report it. Filing frivolous or false reports of copyright infringement can have bad consequences for you.

Chapter 10

Visual Arts

"Visual arts" are things people can look at. While people can of course look at books or clothing or websites, here we'll be considering some traditional—and not so traditional—examples of art forms that must be seen to be appreciated. So we'll consider movies, paintings, sculpture, and photography, but also architecture and landscape design. All of these art forms are primarily visual, and all of them are offered protection by copyright law.

FILM-MAKING

Because they are artistic works in a fixed form, movies are automatically copyrighted when they're created. To be considered "published," they need to be shown to an audience. For a filmmaker, publication means offering copies of their film to theatre owners, retailers, film festivals, or others for the purpose of displaying it—as long as the films being displayed are complete and ready for distribution.[226]

---

[226] US Copyright Office, *Circular 45*: Copyright Registration for Motion Pictures, Including Video Recordings (2014)

Only the final, fixed motion picture (camera work, dialogue, sounds, lighting, special effects, music) can be protected by copyright. It's important to remember that copyright does not protect the *idea* of a movie, or any of the movie's characters. But when a motion picture is published, *all* the components embodied in it are also considered to be published, including the music, the script, and the sounds. For example, a film's screenplay is published to the extent it is contained in the released version of the film.[227] Of course, nothing stops a screenwriter from publishing their screenplay and registering its copyright as a written work. In that case, the film would be a derivative work based on the published screenplay and the screenwriter would need to give the film makers a license to produce the movie based on their screenplay.

Infringement

When making a film, the biggest risk the film maker runs is inadvertently violating other people's copyrights or trademarks. Everything that appears on the screen should be free of copyright or licensed for display. Because one of the sticks in the copyright holder's bundle is the right to display their work. If your movie includes someone else's protected work, you're violating their rights.[228] It may be inadvertent, but it's a violation anyway. That applies to everything from graphics on t-shirts to copies of magazines or books that are visible in the shot to music playing in public places—or even the public places themselves.

I have a personal story about this. Long ago, I was the publisher for a company that published, among other things, textbooks that people used to study for their state real estate license exam. One day I got an email from the producers of *The Sopranos*

---

[227] *Id.*
[228] That's why there's a whole industry dedicated to creating fictional books, magazines, newspapers, and products to take the place of actual, recognizable titles and brands in movies.

asking for permission to use one of our books on the highly successful HBO mobster/family drama. It seems one of the (non-criminal) characters was planning to be a real estate agent, and the producers wanted to show her studying. Naturally, we gave them permission, because no one wants to argue with Tony Soprano.

Documentary Films

Documentaries present a unique challenge for film makers seeking to avoid copyright complications. By their very nature, documentaries deal with the real world, and the real world is full of copyrighted stuff. The principles of fair use (discussed in Chapter 3) apply to documentary films as much as anything else, and really present something of a safe harbor for documentary film makers.

In 2005, the Center for Media and Social Impact published the Documentary Film Maker's Statement of Best Practices in Fair Use (the Statement), a non-binding, non-legal document that established some basic principles for documentary film makers to consider. The Preamble establishes the basic argument:

> *This Statement of Best Practices in Fair Use is necessary because documentary filmmakers have found themselves ... increasingly constrained by demands to clear rights for copyrighted material. Creators in other disciplines do not face such demands to the same extent, and ... documentarians believe that their ability to communicate effectively is being restricted by an overly rigid approach to copyright compliance, and that the public suffers as a result. The knowledge and perspectives that documentarians can provide are compromised by their need to select only the material that copyright holders approve and make available at reasonable prices.*[229]

---

[229] Center for Media and Social Impact, *Documentary Film Maker's Statement of Best Practices in Fair Use*, Preamble,

The Statement describes four common copyright situations faced by documentary film makers:

1. Employing copyrighted material as the object of social, political, or cultural critique;
2. Quoting copyright works of popular culture to illustrate an argument or point;
3. Capturing copyrighted media content in the process of filming something else; and
4. Using copyrighted material in a historical sequence.

The first is clearly critical commentary, and falls squarely into fair use. The second example could be considered a transformative use, since the copyrighted material is not used for its original purpose, but an altogether new one—for instance, using a nonpolitical pop song to ironically comment on a political campaign (a use that could also arguably be considered parody). The third example (illustrated in the case study below) simply refers to the fact that when a documentary film maker points a camera at a city street, for instance, there are going to be copyrighted things caught on film. The documentary is probably not about the movie poster on a theater, but the panning shot across the cityscape clearly shows the poster, and that violates the poster's copyright. Since the only alternative to showing such "accidental" content is to blur the images or superimpose other images over them, the documentary's essential function as reflecting reality accurately would be threatened. The Statement suggests that all such accidentally captured material should be considered fair use, but the law doesn't necessarily agree, and takes a more case-by-case approach. But since fair use exceptions are traditionally available for criticism, comment, news reporting, teaching,

---

https://cmsimpact.org/wp-content/uploads/2016/01/Documentary-Filmmakers.pdf

scholarship, and research,[230] documentaries could be considered analogous to criticism, news reporting, or comment.

Finally, the fourth example involves using copyrighted material in a historical sequence—words, music, photographs, or films that were recorded at the time of an historical event—that are included in a documentary to provide background or historical flavor. For instance, a documentary about 9/11 would need to include news reports, eyewitness accounts caught on audio or video recordings at the time, and video recordings of the events, all of which are subject to copyright protections. However, a 9/11 documentary without those materials would be weak at best. The Statement encourages film makers to use traditional fair use arguments: that the material is tangential to the project and is used only for illustration; that the use is not extensive, and limited to only what is strictly necessary; that the material is unique and vital to the project; that multiple sources are used, and no single copyright source is relied on; that the copyright holders are credited; and that the material either can't be licensed or can only be licensed "on terms that are excessive relative to the reasonable budget" of the film.[231]

It should be noted that the fair use principles and guidelines established in the Statement can also be applied to fictional and experimental film making as well.

Case Study Back in 1999, documentary filmmaker Jon Else made a film, *Sing Faster: The Stagehands' Ring Cycle*, about life backstage at an opera company. In one scene late in the film, some stagehands are backstage during a performance of a Wagner opera, gathered

---

[230] US Copyright Office, "More Information on Fair Use," US Copyright Office Fair Use Index (2021)

[231] Center for Media and Social Impact, *Documentary Film Maker's Statement of Best Practices in Fair Use*, https://cmsimpact.org/wp-content/uploads/2016/01/Documentary-Filmmakers.pdf

around a small TV playing checkers and watching *The Simpsons*.[232]

Obviously, *The Simpsons* is a protected work, so Else had to get permission to use the scene in his movie. Fox, who owns the Simpsons copyright, demanded $10,000 to display the four seconds of the show included in the scene. Because documentaries often have limited budgets, Else decided to replace *The Simpsons* with a scene from a movie he owned. This is clearly an example of the Statement's third situation, but that statement of principle didn't really help Else.

FAN FILMS

Fan films are just what the name suggests: "homemade" movies based on existing franchises. Like fan art and fan fiction, fan films are pretty much per se violations of copyright, because they create derivative works of someone else's copyrighted content without the copyright holder's permission.

That said, the same caveats apply here as to other forms of fan expression: some studios, publishers, and authors take a laissez-faire approach to fan films, seeing them as not much of a threat to the brand and not worth the expense and effort of litigation. Others are not so blasé about it, and will release the legal hounds on unsuspecting fans.

Here's an example of a situation that sort of straddled those two approaches. While it's limited to Star Trek fan films, the cautionary tale and the official guidelines that it resulted in are good for everyone who's thinking of making a fan film to keep in mind.

In 2016, Paramount and CBS Studios, owners of the copyrights and trademarks of the *Star Trek* franchise, sued the creators of

---

[232] Ramsey, Nancy. "The Hidden Cost of Documentaries." The New York Times, October 16, 2005, https://www.nytimes.com/2005/10/16/movies/the-hidden-cost-of-documentaries.html

a planned fan-made movie called *Axanar*. The complaint alleged that

> Defendants have made a short film entitled *Star Trek: Prelude to Axanar*, have written a script for a feature film entitled *Axanar*, and are in the process of producing a film called *Axanar* based on the Axanar Script (collectively the "Axanar Works"). The Axanar Works infringe Plaintiffs' works by using innumerable copyrighted elements of *Star Trek*, including its settings, characters, species, and themes. The Axanar Works are intended to be professional quality productions that, by Defendants' own admission, unabashedly take Paramount's and CBS's intellectual property and aim to "look and feel like a true Star Trek movie." ... Defendants have raised over $1 million so far [through a Kickstarter campaign] to produce these works, including building out a studio and hiring actors, set designers, and costume designers. The Axanar Works are substantially similar to, and unauthorized derivative works of, Plaintiffs' *Star Trek* television series and movies, in contravention of the copyright laws of the United States.[233]

The issue, while not stated outright, is clearly that the *Axanar* creators were planning to launch not a nice little homemade video featuring cardboard sets and filmed in someone's garage, but rather a full-length, high-quality, professional-looking film that would very likely divert revenue from actual *Star Trek* properties. The case was settled before trial, but more importantly it moved Paramount and CBS to create guidelines for fans who were interested in making movies based on their *Star Trek* properties. In a statement announcing the guidelines, the production companies said:

---

[233] *Paramount Pictures v. Axanar Productions*, Case No.: 2:15-cv-09938-RGK-E (USDC, CD CA, 2016)

CBS and Paramount Pictures are big believers in reasonable fan fiction and fan creativity, and, in particular, want amateur fan filmmakers to showcase their passion for *Star Trek*. Therefore, CBS and Paramount Pictures will not object to, or take legal action against, *Star Trek* fan productions that are non-professional and amateur and meet the following guidelines.[234]

Called "Guidelines for Avoiding Objections," the rules limit the scope, length, and budgets of fan-made films based on the franchise, and go into a fair amount of detail, including such requirements as:

- The fan production must be less than 15 minutes for a single self-contained story, or no more than 2 segments, episodes or parts, not to exceed 30 minutes total
- The title of the fan production or any parts cannot include the name "Star Trek." However, the title must contain a subtitle with the phrase: "A STAR TREK FAN PRODUCTION" in plain typeface.
- The content in the fan production must be original, not reproductions, recreations or clips from any Star Trek production.
- The fan production must be a real "fan" production, i.e., creators, actors and all other participants must be amateurs, who aren't compensated for their services.
- The fan production must be non-commercial.
- CBS and Paramount Pictures do not object to limited fundraising for the creation of a fan production, so long as the total amount does not exceed $50,000, including all platform fees, and when the $50,000 goal is reached, all fundraising must cease.
- The fan production must only be exhibited or distributed on a no-charge basis and/or shared via streaming services without generating revenue.

---

[234] https://www.startrek.com/fan-films

- The fan production cannot be distributed in a physical format such as DVD or Blu-ray.
- The fan production cannot be used to derive advertising.
- The fan production must be family friendly and suitable for public presentation. Videos must not include profanity, nudity, obscenity, pornography, depictions of drugs, alcohol, tobacco, or any harmful or illegal activity, or any material that is offensive, fraudulent, defamatory, libelous, disparaging, sexually explicit, threatening, hateful, or any other inappropriate content.
- The fan production must display the following disclaimer in the on-screen credits of the fan productions and on any marketing material including the fan production website or page hosting the fan production:
    - "Star Trek and all related marks, logos and characters are solely owned by CBS Studios Inc. This fan production is not endorsed by, sponsored by, nor affiliated with CBS, Paramount Pictures, or any other Star Trek franchise, and is a non-commercial fan-made film intended for recreational use. No commercial exhibition or distribution is permitted. No alleged independent rights will be asserted against CBS or Paramount Pictures."
- Creators of fan productions must not seek to register their works, nor any elements of the works, under copyright or trademark law.[235]

So to sum up, if you're making a fan film of someone else's copyrighted franchise, be aware that what you are doing is basically an illegal copyright infringement, and none of the standard exceptions will apply to your project. If you're fine with taking that risk, then be sensitive to the fact that you're

---

[235] *Id.*

infringing and keep the Star Trek guidelines in mind: they're probably representative of other studios' feelings on the matter. But remember, regardless of how respectful you are or how pure your motives, you're still breaking the law.

ARCHITECTURE

Copyright protects works that are tangible and fixed, and buildings are certainly tangible and fixed. Architectural works can be protected in two ways: (1) the plans, drawings, model, or elevations can be copyrighted, and (2) the actual physical building itself can be copyrighted. An architectural design can be copyrighted whether or not the building has been, or is ever, actually constructed.[236] This is true for any architectural works created after December 1, 1990. Buildings or building designs published or constructed prior to December 1, 1990 are not protected by copyright.[237]

An architect can register[238] a copyright for an architectural work if it is "a humanly habitable structure that is intended to be both permanent and stationary."[239] So houses, office buildings, hotels—any structure that people are expected to inhabit—can be copyrighted. (Roads, bridges, and other structures not intended for people to spend time in, on the other hand, are not copyrightable.) The copyright includes front, rear, and side facades as well as interior walls that define the space. However, normal architectural elements such as windows and doors, room configurations, lighting, and furniture placement are not covered by copyright.[240]

---

[236] *Id.*
[237] 37 CFR § 202.11(d)(3)(i)
[238] See Chapter 13 for registration tips
[239] US Copyright Office, Circular 41: *Copyright Protection of Architectural Works* (rev. 2021)
[240] US Copyright, Circular 40: Copyright Registration for Pictorial, Graphic, and Sculptural Works, §926.2 (rev. 2021)

There are limitations here, though, not only for architects. The architectural copyright doesn't just prevent an architect from copying someone else's design; it protects *the building itself*. In a bit of a deviation from normal copyright—where only the copyright holder is allowed to make major changes to the work--the owner of an architectural work (that is, the building's owner, who may not be the architect/copyright holder), is free to alter the building or even have it destroyed without the architect's consent.[241] Although, really, that's not exactly a departure from copyright law: consider it the skyscraper equivalent of the first sale doctrine.

An architectural work is considered to be "published" for copyright registration purposes when its plans or drawings are made available to the public by sale or transfer. While it might make logical sense, construction of a building is not considered "publication" for purposes of registration.[242]

GARDENING/LANDSCAPING[243]

If you're a landscape designer, the plans for your landscapes are copyrightable. But the actual garden you've designed…not so much. The reason is pretty obvious, if you think about it. Copyright requires that the work be in a tangible, permanent form, and plants—by their nature—are not permanent. Even perennials come and go with the seasons, and change their appearance.

You should be specific in any agreements with clients regarding who owns the plans: it's very easy to interpret a landscape designer's drawings for a specific customer's property to be a work for hire. Your contract should clearly state that you own the plans, although the garden belongs to the property owner.

---

[241] USC § 120 (b)
[242] 37 CFR § 202.11(c)(5).
[243] See "Plant Patents" in Chapter 16.

This was made clear in a case called *Kelley v. Chicago Park District*. In that case, Chapman Kelley, a nationally recognized artist known for his representational paintings of romantic floral and woodland interpretations set within ellipses, received permission from the Chicago Park District to install wildflower display at the north end of Grant Park in the heart of downtown Chicago.[244] "Wildflower Works" was composed of two huge oval flower beds, each nearly as big as a football field and covering 1.5 acres of lakefront park, featuring a variety of native wildflowers.[245] Promoted as "living art," Wildflower Works received critical and popular acclaim, and for a while Kelley and a group of volunteers tended the vast garden:[246]

They pruned and weeded and regularly planted new seeds, both to experiment with the garden's composition and to fill in where initial specimen had not flourished. Of course, the forces of nature—the varying bloom periods of the plants; their spread habits, compatibility, and life cycles; and the weather—produced constant change. Some wildflowers naturally did better than others. Some spread aggressively and encroached on neighboring plants. Some withered and died. Unwanted plants sprung up from seeds brought in by birds and the wind. Insects, rabbits, and weeds settled in, eventually taking a toll.[247]

But by 2004 Wildflower Works had deteriorated and the City's goals for Grant Park had changed, so the Park District dramatically modified the garden by reducing its size, turning the oval flower beds into rectangles, and changing some of the plants.[248] Kelley sued the Park District for violating his moral rights under VARA.[249] He claimed that Wildflower Works was a "work of visual art" under VARA, and that the Park District's reconfiguration of it was an intentional "distortion, mutilation,

---

[244] *Kelley v. Chicago Park District*, 635 F.3d 290 (7th Cir. 2011)
[245] *Id.*
[246] *Id.*
[247] *Id.*
[248] *Id.*
[249] 17 USC § 106A; See Chapter 1

or other modification" of his work and was "prejudicial to his . . . honor or reputation." Kelley sued the Park District for violating his "right of integrity" under the Visual Artists Rights Act of 1990 ("VARA") discussed in Chapter 2.

The trial court rejected Kelley's copyright claim, and the court of appeals affirmed that "for reasons relating to copyright's requirements of expressive authorship and fixation, a living garden like Wildflower Works is not copyrightable."[250] In plain English, that means that no matter how pretty or creative, a garden changes over time (so it's not "fixed"), and because it's not a painting or sculpture it fails to qualify for "authorship" protections under VARA.

The bottom line for landscape designers and creative gardeners: Your plans and diagrams are copyrightable and protected, but not their physical expression. If you design a front yard for a client, there is nothing to stop a passer-by from copying it exactly in their own yard.

PAINTINGS & SCULPTURE

Paintings and sculptures are explicitly copyrightable under the Copyright Act. In fact, visual artists have additional legal protections under the Visual Artists Rights Act (VARA) of 1990.[251] VARA guarantees that artists have the right to both be recognized as the author of their work and to have their name removed from works that in their view have been modified, distorted, or mutilated in a way that "would be prejudicial to his or her honor or reputation."[252]

Paintings

When someone purchases a painting, it's really no different than if they purchased a book; the artist still holds the copyright of

---

[250] *Kelley*
[251] 17 USC § 106a
[252] 17 USC § 106a(3)A

the work, while the collector is entitled to display, sell, or destroy the work under the First Sale Doctrine, but they can't sell copies of it. On the other hand, if an artwork is mutilated, damaged, or altered the artist can "disown" it, which would probably have a negative effect on its value.

If the work is "famous" the artist can actually prevent the collector from tampering with it at all, regardless of the First Sale Doctrine—probably on the basis that there is a public interest in the preservation of recognized art. An artist can also reproduce the painting or sculpture, or sell photos of it, since they still hold copyright. The collector isn't entitled to own the only existing copy.

VARA's protections aren't 100%, however. If the collector is going to display the artwork in a way that the artist doesn't approve of—but that won't destroy or mutilate or modify the art—there's nothing the artist can do about it. So, for instance, Susan Sculptor carved a beautiful statue of a man celebrating a victory. A collector purchases the statue, and has it displayed in the lobby of an organization dedicated to everything the artist is against. The artist has a First Amendment right to speak out against the display, but no right under copyright law to prevent it, even though the display is "prejudicial to his or her honor or reputation."[253]

VARA provides an interesting twist on the "first sale doctrine" already discussed in Chapter 1. There, I said that once an author/artist sells a copy of his or her work to someone, they have no further rights in that copy (other than copyright), and have no control over what buyers do with their copies. VARA clarifies that that's not entirely true; in the case of some works of visual art, the artist's rights in how the work is treated continue even after purchase.

This has come up with my own photography. My license agreement with models permits them to freely post images

---

[253] 17 USC § 106c(3)

online as long as they attribute them to me. But occasionally a model will decide to add a filter or other effect to the photo before sharing it on social media. In those cases, I have asked the model to remove my name from the post, because what they're displaying is not representative of the quality of my work.

Sculpture

Original sculptural works are specifically covered by copyright law.[254] "Sculptures" are two- or three-dimensional pieces such as carvings, ceramics, figurines, or maquettes;[255] works that are molded, modeled, cast, carved, compiled, or constructed; and may be freestanding or relief. The definition of "sculpture" for purposes of copyright law isn't limited to heroic figures carved out of blocks of marble, or massive sheets of iron welded together to depict man's inhumanity to man: rather, the Copyright Office also identifies the following as "sculptures:"

- Toys
- Dolls
- Molds
- Bas-reliefs

Like any other copyrightable work, sculptors hold copyright as soon as their work is in some tangible form. Copyright adheres at all stages of sculptural work: a rough conceptual sketch, a final detailed drawing, and a completed sculpture are all protected by the artist's copyright. However, also like any other copyrightable work, the sculptor's copyright is stronger if it's registered with the US Copyright Office.

When submitting a sculptural work for copyright registration, the usual requirement that a copy of the work be included in the submission is waived. Instead, applicants can submit a photo of the sculpture—but be sure to clearly identify the nature of the

---

[254] 17 USC § 102 (a) (5) "pictorial, graphic, and sculptural works"
[255] US Copyright Office, *Circular 40*: Copyright Registration for Works of the Visual Arts (rev'd 2015)

work as "sculpture" in the application, because otherwise the Copyright Office might think you wanted to copyright the photograph.[1]

Note that a sculpture that is based on a non-sculptural copyrighted work infringes on that original work's copyright unless the sculptor has obtained the copyright holder's permission. (See the Koons Case Study in Chapter 3)

Sculptural items that are part of a useful item are still copyrightable on their own, even though the useful item is not. For instance, statuettes designed to be lampstands can still be copyrighted separately from their utilitarian function.[256] It's important to remember, though, that only those statuettes are copyrighted, not the *idea* of statuettes-as-lampstands.[257] While the copyright will prevent others from using those same statuettes as lampstands, it won't stop anyone from using different statuettes in the same way.

PHOTOGRAPHY

The US copyright law protects photographs as pictorial works.[258]

To be protected by copyright, though, the photograph must display some degree of creative expression. In photography, creative uniqueness is achieved through the photographer's choices in such things as

- Subject matter
- Angle
- Lighting
- Exposure
- Lenses
- Editing

Photography is an extremely personal art form. That is, even if a dozen people take a photo of an object at the same time, each

---

[256] *Mazer v. Stein*, 347 US 201, 74 S.Ct. 460, 98 L.Ed. 630 (1954)
[257] *Id.*
[258] US Copyright Office, *Compendium*, Chapter 900: Jewelry, § 909 (rev'd 2021)

photo will be subtly different simply depending on where each photographer was standing. The laws of physics being what they are, no two photographers can occupy exactly the same spot at exactly the same time, so off the bat the images will not be identical.

Subject Matter of Photographs: Creativity

There is no legal requirement that the subject of a photograph must be eligible for copyright protection. A photo of an object or scene that is in the public domain is still copyrightable as a photograph—as long as there was some creative effort on the part of the photographer.[259]

For instance, a photographer who takes a photo of the St. Louis Arch is not claiming copyright in the Arch, but only in the photo of it, for which the photographer selected the camera, the time of day, the angle, and composition. On the other hand, a photograph of a contemporary artist's painting, where the painting fills the frame and where lighting and editing were done solely to reproduce the painting exactly, is not eligible for copyright because there's no creative effort by the artist. [260] (Also, the photographer has violated the painter's copyright.)

Here's a personal example. I took this photograph:[261]

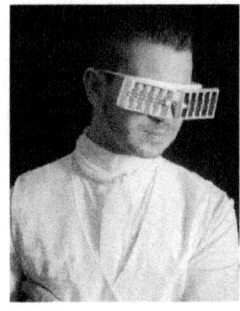

---

[259] *Id.*, § 909.2
[260] See, e.g., *Bridgeman Art Library v. Corel Corp.*, 36 F. Supp. 2d 191 (S.D.N.Y. 1999)
[261] Photograph copyright © Evan Butterfield; Model: Louis D'Aprile

I own the copyright to this photo, which means no one gets to reproduce it without my permission (for the record, I gave myself permission to use it in this book). I created the weird glasses the model is wearing, so I own the copyright on that aspect of the image as well.

What I don't own is Gillette's intellectual property rights on the razor cartridge holders that the glasses are made out of; but that's a pretty darned transformative use (razor holders into fashionable eyewear), so I'm covered under fair use for copyright, and their patent is secure. I also don't own any rights in the clothing the model is wearing, but we've discussed the challenges of useful items previously, so it's not a worry. In this case, the model doesn't own the rights to his own image, because he signed a licensing agreement with me before the shoot that gives the photographer all the rights.

Subject Matter of Photographs: Buildings

Copyright law specifically permits individuals to photograph, paint, or make sketches of a building if it's in a publicly-visible place:

> The copyright in an architectural work that has been constructed does not include the right to prevent the making, distributing, or public display of pictures, paintings, photographs, or other pictorial representations of the work, if the building in which the work is embodied is located in or ordinarily visible from a public place. [262]

Photos of such a building can be legally made, distributed, and displayed without the copyright holder's consent.[263]

But again, nothing's so simple. For example, a photographer takes a picture of a Las Vegas casino property. First thing, it matters where the photographer is standing. If they stood in a

---

[262] 17 USC § 120 (a)
[263] *Id.*

public park across the street from the casino to take the picture, they're fine. If they were standing on the casino's privately-owned parking lot, they may encounter legal issues. They can post the photo on their website, or make a print and display it at a showing. But if they proceed to *sell* the photo or includes it in a commercial collection of her work, they have gone beyond fair use and is infringing the building's copyright.

Trademark law includes protections for logos. If a photo of a casino includes the casino's registered trademark, things may get complicated. For the photographer to use an image of private property commercially, a release should be obtained from the property owner. That will eliminate unpleasant lawsuits later.

The bottom line is very similar to the bottom line for Internet images: Just because you can freely see it doesn't mean it's yours to do with as you please.

Subject Matter of Photographs: People

Obviously if you're a portrait photographer and someone comes to your studio to have headshots done, you own the copyright. Although a client comes to a photographer for a portrait and pays for the service, the photograph is not considered a work for hire (in which case the client would own copyright). But a client isn't an employer, and a portrait photographer is more like an independent contractor,[264] so the photographer holds the copyright. The same is true for an editorial or art photographer: just because a model pays you for a specific shoot doesn't make them the owner of the copyright in your creative work.

It gets trickier though, with street photography, which involves taking photographs of people in public places, usually without their knowledge or permission, for purposes of realism. Because

---

[264] See, e.g., *Community for Creative Non-Violence v. Reid*, 490 US 730 (1989) Sculptor retained by organization to create sculpture was not an employee.

public spaces are public, people in public spaces don't have what the law calls a "reasonable expectation of privacy."[265] That just means that if you're sitting in your living room you don't expect anyone to take your picture or listen to your conversations. But if you're in a public park, or walking down a crowded city street, or eating at a busy outdoor café, you really can't expect to have any privacy. So again, street photographers can take photos of strangers walking down the street or playing on the beach or surfing or having a picnic in the park.

The tricky bit arises after that picture is taken. While the photographer owns the copyright and all the bundle of sticks that comes with it, they don't "own" the person who's in the picture, or their likeness. So be careful with what you do with your street photography:

- You can post your photos in your online gallery, or make prints of and display them in a gallery.
- You can probably sell the photos to individual collectors.
- You probably can't license the photos to commercial entities or stock photography sites, because you can't control what happens to them, which brings us to the main thing:
- You can't do anything with the photo that suggests anything about the character of an identifiable person in that photo.

Right to Privacy

First off, while most Americans would say their right to privacy is one of their most treasured rights, there is no right to privacy expressed in the Constitution. Rather, the Supreme Court has found an *implied* right to privacy by squinting at the Constitution and looking for "emanations" from the ideas of the

---

[265] *Katz v. United States*, 389 US 347 (1967)(J. Harlan, concurring) Person in a telephone booth had a reasonable expectation of privacy.

1st, 3rd, 4th, 5th, 9th, and 14th Amendments.[266] Basically, the Court found that the various guarantees in the Bill of Rights create specific zones of privacy for specific activities, and when you stitch all those zones together you get a general Constitutional right to privacy. The expectation of privacy, however, is a sliding scale that varies depending on where you are. You have a total right to privacy in your own home, for instance; less of a right to privacy when you're in your car, and should have virtually no expectation of privacy when you're eating in a restaurant or walking in a park, playing volleyball on the beach, enjoying a concert, or marching in a protest demonstration.

As a general rule, the privacy right (like other rights in the Constitution) has more to do with the *government's* actions than those of an individual.[267] However, if you're taking photographs in a park or on a beach or at a political rally, you don't need to obtain signed releases from anyone who happens to be in your photo. Your pictures are of places or events, not necessarily specific individuals, and even the specific individuals are in public and have no expectation of privacy.[268] If someone asks that you not take their picture or video them in a public place, it's polite to comply, but it's not legally mandatory and you're under no obligation to stop.

An individual's right to privacy *can* be violated by someone—and the individual can sue for damages—if the photographer's activity presents them in, for instance, a false light. For example, a street photographer takes a photo of a person walking alone on a path in a public park. The person's face is visible and

---

[266] *Griswold v. Connecticut*, 381 US 479 (1965). The privacy right as found by Griswold has been potentially called into question by the US Supreme Court's decision in *Dobbs v. Jackson Women's Health Organization* (2022).

[267] That is, the First Amendment right to free speech means the *government* can't prevent you from speaking or deny you a platform; however, private companies and individuals are not prohibited from preventing you from expressing your opinion.

identifiable, but the photo is really about the path and the park. The photographer licenses the photo to a nonprofit dedicated to curing a terrible, embarrassing, and highly contagious disease. Of course one of the sticks in the photographer's copyright bundle is the right to do license or sell images. But if the nonprofit proceeds to post the photo on billboards throughout the city with the slogan "Don't Let A Terrible and Highly Contagious Disease Make You Lonely," the subject of the street photograph can sue the photographer *and* the nonprofit for false light, because everyone will think that they suffer from the disease. That's a pretty extreme example, but the principle holds true for any use of a person's image that suggests anything untrue about them.

So the bottom line with taking photos of people in public places is that the usual copyrights are a little bit reduced by the privacy rights of your subjects.

 **So what do you take away from all this? Four simple points to remember:**

1. In film-making, be careful not to violate other people's copyrights or trademarks, especially in street scenes.
2. If you're taking photographs in public place, you don't need to obtain signed releases from random people who happen to be in your photo: as long as they're not the main subject of your photo, they have no reasonable expectation of privacy.
3. Plans and diagrams for gardens and landscapes are copyrightable and protected, but not the gardens and landscapes themselves.
4. A photo of an object or scene that is in the public domain is still copyrightable as a photograph—as long as there was some creative effort on the part of the photographer.

Chapter 11

Technology

COMPUTER PROGRAMS AND GAMES

Programs

The US Copyright Office defines a computer program as "a set of statements or instructions to be used directly or indirectly in a computer to bring about a certain result."[269]

A computer program is similar to a literary work: it uses language to create a result. While computers are "useful articles" in that they are machines that perform operations, their underlying programming is the result of human creative effort. Copyright protection for a computer program extends to all of the copyrightable expression embodied in the program, although copyright law does not protect the functional aspects of a computer program, such as the program's algorithms, formatting, functions, logic, or system design.[270]

There are two kinds of code in a program: source code and object code. Source code is essentially what the programmer

---

[269] US Copyright Office, *Circular 61*: Copyright Registration of Computer Programs (rev. 2021)
[270] *Id.*

writes, in a particular programming language. It's human-readable by people who know how to read that code. Object code, on the other hand, is what the computer "reads" to understand and carry out the program. Object code is a translation of source code, and they both say the same thing, just in ways that are understandable by two different audiences. Either the source code or the object code can be copyrighted, but not both, because they're the same thing.[271]

Games

Copyright law protects computer programs as original works of authorship, and computer games are basically elaborate computer programs. Essentially, you can copyright your code, the rendering of characters and scenery; the specific storyline of the game[272]; and any original music you include.[273]

That said, there are elements of computer games that are not protectible by copyright. Primarily, these are things referred to as *scènes à faire*, which we discussed earlier: those elements in a story (or game) that have to be there in order for the game to be recognized as part of a specific genre. For computer games, those elements might include spaceships, FTL drives, and aliens in a sci-fi shooter; wizards and dragons and castles in a fantasy RPG; cowboys and horses in a Western; bodices to be ripped and

---

[271] US Copyright Office, *Compendium*, Chapter 900: Visual Art Works, § 721.5

[272] That is, you *can't* copyright "a space adventure battling aliens," because that can apply generically to lots of games; you *can* copyright "a story about beautiful space pirate Asteroid Annie and her adventures aboard the Starship *Wonder-Bob* fighting the Wicked Space Baron Alquazar from the Planet Noomie-7, including quests to interplanetary trading posts and encounters with interplanetary hooligans, con-men, reprobates, and kindly scientists."

[273] For individual characters, you might explore trademarking them as opposed to copyright. Trademark usually offers more protection for character designs.

swordfights to be had in a romance. Those elements are considered generic, and aren't copyrightable.

So if you develop a space shooter game involving waves of aliens attacking the player's spaceship, you can't sue someone else who develops a space shooter involving waves of aliens attacking the player's spaceship. Your copyright protects the look and feel and unique gaming elements of your game, but you don't own the genre. On the other hand, how you express those elements is protectable. So if your space shooter features starships that look like a combination housekey/hairbrush/toilet plunger/stapler, and you later find a new space shooter game that features an identical starship, you will likely be able to successfully sue for copyright infringement, even though "starships" are *scènes à faire* for space shooters.

PODCASTS

Podcasts are protectable by copyright as creative or expressive works. Specifically, podcasts are considered "sound recordings" under copyright law: "works that result from the fixation of a series of musical, spoken, or other sounds."[274] We'll talk about the potential challenge created by those "other sounds" in a podcast in a moment.

For podcasters, your written script is copyrightable as well as the sound recording of your actual podcast. Because of their digital (and therefore easily shareable) nature, it's a good idea to state the copyright status of your podcast at the beginning or end. A simple "Copyright 2022 by P. Odcaster" is sufficient. Adding a statement like "all rights reserved" means that you are not giving anyone a license to do anything with your podcast other than listen to it. (You may need to give the delivery platform a license, of course, but that will likely be included in the platform's terms of service.)

---

[274] 17 USC §101

It's important to remember that ideas are not protectable by copyright. So while the *content* of your podcast is protected, the *idea* behind it is not. For instance, assume you decide to make a podcast series devoted to an episode-by-episode analysis of the long-running TV series, *The Golden Girls* (1985-1992). Because you're engaging in what amounts to criticism, you're entitled to make specific references to the series, its characters, and stories. Each episode of your podcast is copyrighted by you, and protected from infringement. But what's not protected is your *idea*. Nothing will prevent another podcaster from dedicating a podcast to an episode-by-episode analysis of *The Golden Girls*, so don't even try to stop them.

Interviews

Many podcasts include interviews, and that gets a little complicated under copyright law. Basically, you own your questions and follow-up comments, but the person you're interviewing holds the copyright to their answers. That's because the answers are their own words, reflecting their own opinions: just the stuff copyright is meant to protect. So it's good practice to obtain a written release from interviewees that gives you permission to include their words in your podcast.

Also, if you're going to edit the interview in a way that touches their answers, it's just polite (as well as legally safer) to share the edited version with the interviewee for their approval. (Note that while the interviewee "owns" their answers, you still hold copyright to the entire podcast, including the interview.)

"Other Sounds"

A common pitfall for podcasters is theme music. Despite common opinions, there is no thirty-second "safe harbor" for using just a short clip of a copyrighted song as your podcast theme. Unless you're using your own composition or music that is in the public domain—either because its copyright has lapsed or because it's open access—you cannot use other people's copyrighted musical compositions without a license from them. So don't.

Similarly, (and sticking with our *Golden Girls* podcast example) you don't have the right to use audio clips from the show, or its theme song, without permission from the copyright holders. To use a real-life example, two of the actors who appeared in *Star Trek: Voyager*, Garrett Wang and Robert Duncan McNeill, have a podcast in which they discuss each episode of the show, reminisce about their experiences, and discuss filming, directing, acting, and production details. Despite their connection to *Star Trek: Voyager*, though, their podcast uses public domain theme music, and they never include audio clips from the shows. So if two podcasters who were actually *in* the show they're discussing can't use clips, probably neither should you.

WEBSITES

If you manage a website that allows users to comment, post reviews, or otherwise publish content, you run the risk that they will post content that infringes on others' copyrights. Until Congress passed the Digital Millennium Copyright Act (DMCA), websites could be held liable for content posted by users, whether or not the website operator knew that the content was infringing, or even that it was posted on the site. DMCA safe harbor provisions protect website owners from being sued by copyright holders when site users publish infringing material. They are expected, however, to remove infringing content when its presence is brought to their attention.

Of course, DMCA doesn't protect the owner of a website from being sued for copyright infringement if they post infringing content on their site themselves. Keep that in mind when you're selecting images especially.

 **So what do you take away from all this? Four simple points to remember:**

1. Computer programs are copyrightable, but only either the source code or the object code can be protected, not both.
2. *Scènes à faire*—those elements in a game that have to be there in order for the game to be recognized as part of a specific genre—can't be copyrighted.
3. In interviews, you as interviewer may own the copyright to the interaction, but the person being interviewed owns the copyright to their own words.
4. The "safe harbor" provision of the DMCA protects website owners from being sued by copyright holders if site users publish infringing material—as long as the infringing content is removed promptly when the site owner is notified.

Chapter 12

Writing

LITERARY WORKS

The Copyright Act explicitly protects "literary works," and doesn't distinguish among poetry and prose, or poetry, fiction, and nonfiction.[275] The Copyright Office provides this nonexclusive list of examples of the types of things it considers "literary works:"

> Fiction, nonfiction, poetry, serial publications (e.g., newspapers, magazines, etc.), articles, advertising copy, written communications (e.g., letters, email messages), reference works, directories, catalogs, compilations of information, computer programs, databases, e-books, audiobooks, online textual works (e.g., blogs, website text), and similar types of textual works.[276]

Nonetheless, we'll look at poetry, fiction (with a special focus on fan-fiction), and nonfiction separately, because they each have their own wrinkles to consider.

---

[275] 17 USC § 101
[276] US Copyright Office, *Compendium*: Visual Art Works Chapter 500, §503.1B (rev. 2021)

FICTION

Once upon a time, an author wrote a novel. It was not a good novel, to be honest; in fact, it was very, very bad. But on that dark and stormy night, the author sat themselves down and wrote their novel. They might have written a children's story, or a short story. It doesn't matter—they wrote the thing, which in this case was a novel. Copyright doesn't care about the quality or character of a work, just the fact that it exists.

The novel was about mysterious goings-on in a dinosaur zoo (in the novel's reality, dinosaurs hadn't become extinct but continued to live on isolated islands). Now, this may sound very similar to another novel (and series of movies) about a dinosaur zoo of sorts, but remember: *ideas* can't be copyrighted, just the way those ideas are *expressed*. As long as the author's novel steered clear of story and character elements associated with *Jurassic Park*, a dinosaur zoo is a fine thing to write about, and won't attract cease and desist letters from Michael Crichton or the Knopf company.[277] Of course, it would have been better to have written about a wholly unique thing, but there are only so many wholly unique things in the world to write about, after all, and dinosaur zoos are certainly interesting.

In one case highly relevant to this situation, the author of *Jurassic Park* sued the author of a series of children's books, alleging that the books copied his novel. The court examined seven factors (total concept and feel, theme, setting, time sequence, pace, characters, and sequence of events) and found that only one of them—the setting, in a dinosaur zoo—was substantially similar between the two books, and that factor was non-copyrightable as a *scene a faire*.[278] Also, Crichton's book was over 700 pages, and the four children's books were each no

---

[277] See, e.g., *Williams v. Crichton*, 860 F. Supp. 158 (S.D.N.Y. 1994)
[278] See Chapter 2.

more than 30 pages.[279] However, the comparative length of the works is not as important as the amount of content allegedly copied. If the children's book had included 30 pages of direct copying of *Jurassic Park*, the result would have certainly been different.

The trick is to avoid being found to be "substantially similar" to an existing work. The test for substantial similarity is "whether an average lay observer would recognize the alleged copy as having been appropriated from the copyrighted work."[280]

The main copyright issue for fiction writers, however, shouldn't be how much or how closely to crib from an existing work.

Characters in a fictional work may or may not be eligible for copyright, depending on how unique they are. "[T]he less developed the characters, the less they can be copyrighted; that is the penalty an author must bear for marking them too indistinctly."[281] That is, if your characters are stereotypes or nondescript vehicles for plot or dialog, they aren't eligible for copyright protection. Remember, though, that your whole work of fiction *is* copyrighted and can be registered with the Copyright Office, and that copyright for the work as a whole will necessarily include the characters. However, to protect the characters themselves, you need a separate copyright for them, and that's where the whole uniqueness thing comes in.

"The copyright in the registered work protects the author's expression of the character, but it does not protect the mere concept of the character. The copyright in the character itself is

---

[279] *Id.*, See also *Allen v. Scholastic, Inc.*, 739 F. Supp. 2d 642 (S.D.N.Y. 2011): using a similar set of comparisons, the court determined that a 16-page children's book about a boy wizard, *The Adventures of Willy the Wizard — No 1 Livid Land*, did not violate the copyright of the 700-page *Harry Potter and the Goblet of Fire*.
[280] *Ideal Toy Corp. v. Fab-Lu, Ltd.*, 360 F.2d 1021, 1022 (2d Cir.1966)
[281] *Nichols v. Universal Pictures Corp.*, 45 F.2d 119 (2d Cir. 1930)

limited to the artistic rendition of the character...in textual form."[282]

So the bottom line is you can have your characters copyrighted separately—just like Mickey Mouse or James Bond or Wonder Woman or Homer Simpson—as long as your characters are as unique, identifiable, developed, and recognizable as those characters are. If you plan to use your fictional characters on t-shirts and coffee mugs, getting them copyrighted separately makes good sense.

Defamation

As we get ready to turn our attention to nonfiction literary works, there's one area where fiction and nonfiction overlap: reality. Many fiction writers like to include real people or places in their work. That's an attractive option, because readers will immediately recognize the setting or person and fill in the blanks in any descriptions or narrative with their own impressions. The challenge here is that sometimes neither places nor people are pleased with how they are depicted in a fiction work. We're talking here about defamation.

There's always a delicate balance between one person's right to freedom of speech and another's right to protect their good name. It can be hard to know which personal remarks are proper and which fall into the categories of defamation, libel, and slander.

Defamation is a term that covers any statement that hurts someone's reputation. If the statement is made *in writing and published*, the defamation is called **libel**. If the hurtful statement is *spoken* in the presence of a third party (or if it's broadcast) the statement is **slander**. Spoken words often fade more quickly from memory, so slander is generally considered less serious

---

[282] US Copyright Office, *Compendium*: Copyrightable Authorship: What Can Be Registered, Chapter 300, §313.4(H)

than libel. In other words, defamation is the offense; libel and slander are the way the offense was carried out.

Because freedom of speech is enshrined in the US Constitution (just like copyright), it's not easy to successfully claim defamation. To prove defamation, a plaintiff has to show all of the following factors:

1. Someone made a statement;
2. The statement was published;
3. The statement caused a specific injury to the plaintiff or their reputation;
4. The statement was false; and
5. The statement did not fall into a privileged category.

Number 4 is particularly interesting. The law will only consider a statement defamatory if it is actually false. A true statement is not considered defamation. (Statements of opinion are not considered false because they are subjective by their nature.) But the burden of proving that the statement was true is on the defendant. Truth is a complete defense to a charge of defamation. As long as the defendant can prove the general truth of a statement—even if at the time they made the statement they didn't know whether it was true or not—they will not be liable for defamation.

Public Figures

Courts have determined that public figures can only win a defamation suit when the statement that was made was published with the actual intention of harming the public figure. To prove that, the public figure has to prove that the author knew the statement was untrue when they made it, and had "reckless disregard" for whether or not it was true.

Defamation per se

Some statements are so defamatory that they are considered defamation per se ("of itself"). Most states in the US have defamation per se laws on their books. Under defamation per se, the plaintiff does not have to prove that the statements harmed their reputation, just that they were made publicly. Only certain statements are subject to defamation per se:

- Allegation of a serious criminal misbehavior
- Claims of professional incompetence
- Assertion of serious sexual misconduct (historically, unchastity in women); or
- Declaration that someone is suffering from a "loathsome disease" (historically, this refers to sexually transmitted diseases)

The general rule for writing about real people (or real places) in fiction or nonfiction works is stick to the truth. If you need someone to be a nasty villain, make up a nasty villain instead of using a real person. And don't just change the name of the real person, or tweak their description slightly: if they're recognizable from your work, you may be liable for libel.

But bringing us back to copyright specifically, there doesn't seem to be anything in copyright law that requires a work to be free of defamatory statements in order to be copyrighted. As long as the libel is original and unique, it can be copyrighted. Copyright won't protect against a defamation lawsuit, however.

FAN FICTION

Like fan art, fan fiction is absolutely a violation of copyright. Because it uses characters, settings, and situations that must be recognizably drawn from protected works, fair use exceptions just don't apply. So how can there be so much fan fiction on fan sites all over the Internet?

As of this publication, the website fanfiction.net has indexed an enormous number of works of fan fiction.[283] The chart below

---

[283] www.fanfiction.net

barely scratches the surface of what fanfiction.net has collected, and just by itself represents nearly 2 million works of fan fiction!

FRANCHISE	FAN FICTION
Harry Potter	839K
Naruto	437K
Twilight	222K
Pokémon	102K
Yu-Gi-Oh	68.4K
Lord of the Rings	58.0K
Star Wars	57.5K
Dragon Ball Z	53.9K
Hunger Games	46.2K
Batman	19.7K
South Park	19.4K
Star Trek	14.3K
X-Men	13.6K
Doctor Who	13.0K
Buffy the Vampire Slayer	8.7K
Spider-Man	8.2K

If all of that is illegal, how can fan fiction exist?

Like fan art, the answer is simple: tolerance. Some studios, publishers, and authors are perfectly happy to let peoples' imaginations run wild with the characters and worlds they've created. That may be because of respect for their fans, or indifference, or it may be because pursuing infringement lawsuits against individuals is expensive and time-consuming, and is generally not a good look with the people who flock to your movies and buy your books.

J.K. Rowling, for instance, is generally very tolerant of fan fiction as long as it's respectful of her characters and stories, and shows up only on fan websites and not for sale (see Warner Bros. Entertainment Inc. v. RDR Books in Chapter 2). Rowling is on record as not being especially delighted with "slash fiction"—erotic treatments of her characters. George R.R. Martin and Anne Rice, on the other hand, have strongly discouraged any fan art and fan fiction based on their works.

If you're writing and publishing fan fiction, be aware that you are absolutely positively infringing someone's copyright. Chances are no one will care, but you don't want to be on the receiving end of a giant publisher's cease and desist letter.

NONFICTION

Like any other creative work, works of nonfiction are copyrighted when they are created. There are a few things to watch out for in writing nonfiction works, however, none of which are unique to nonfiction, but all of which pose special risks for nonfiction writers.

The nature of nonfiction works is that they are based on real events, real places, and real people. Each of those characteristics poses a unique copyright challenge for nonfiction writers.

Real Events

When journalists arrives at the site of an automobile accident, their coverage of the accident is protected by copyright. The accident itself, however, is a thing that actually happened, plainly visible to the public, and so is in the public domain. If a nonfiction writer produces an original work about the accident based on having witnessed it themselves, or on talking to people who witnessed it, their work is protected. On the other hand, if they reproduce the story written by the journalists, they are violating copyright.

Similarly, if an author writes a history of the Vietnam War based on interviews with veterans among their family and friends, that original work is all theirs. If they write their history using other people's copyrighted histories of the Vietnam war, they need to be careful to cite sources and bring as much original research, observation, and analysis to the table as possible. There are two reasons for that: first, using other people's work without citation is clear copyright infringement (it may be infringement even with citation, if the actual words are reproduced in a large quantity). Second, it will just be a more interesting book for readers, and be more widely read, if what it offers is more original than simply regurgitated from other works.

Real Places

There is a risk, when writing about real places such as stores or restaurants, that the store or restaurant won't much care for what you've written. Nonfiction writers need to be careful not to use real, privately-owned locations in a way that could be construed as libelous (see above). For instance, alleging that a particular restaurant in a specific town is a bubbling cauldron of ptomaine would risk a defamation suit from the owners.

Real People

With regard to how to write about real people in a nonfiction work, stick to the provably true. If what you're writing about someone is factually true—and its truth can be demonstrated—you have no worries. When you have to suggest what went on behind closed doors, or in someone's mind, be very careful to stay as close to the truth as possible. Naturally, if you write things about a real person that are untrue but flattering and complimentary, they're probably not going to sue you for defamation. But stick to the truth, even though lies are copyrightable too.

POETRY

If you write your poem on paper
Or on a screen with bits of light
Or carve it on a marble slab
It's still your copyright.

The format doesn't matter
And the media matters not
And neither does the metric style;
Copyright is what you've got.

So you can write a haiku
Or a limerick or a sonnet
Free verse, epic, rhymed or blank—
Your copyright's what is on it.

From the moment that you write it
It's protected by the C
It can't be distributed by others
Or reproduced by me.

But if your poem includes some words
From another poet's poesy,

Have a license or be transformative

Or to court you'll have to mosey.

And if you write a *bunch* of poems

Please don't express frustration;

You can bundle them together

In a single registration.[284]

 **So what do you take away from all this? Four simple points to remember:**

1. While ideas can't be copyrighted, authors should avoid plots and characters that are "substantially similar" to copyrighted works.
2. Public figures can only prevail in a defamation lawsuit if they can prove that a false statement about them was published with the actual intention of causing them harm.
3. Nonfiction writers should be careful not to use real people and privately-owned locations in a way that could be construed as libelous.
4. Collected works of poetry, fiction, or nonfiction can be registered as a single work if they have a common author and are in the same medium.

---

[284] I apologize for writing the Poetry discussion as a poem. Sometimes I can't help myself.

PART 3

PROTECT YOUR CREATIVE WORK

As we've seen, there are many ways to protect your creative work. In this final part of the book, we'll turn our attention to the practical considerations you should keep in mind when considering things like whether or not to register your copyright; whether to enforce your copyright at all or just let your work be free in the world; and how trademark may offer an alternative for some creatives. Finally, we'll review some basics of contract law, because written contracts are how you license your work and let other people use the sticks in your bundle.

Chapter 13
Registering Your Copyright

Way back in Chapter 1, we learned that copyright exists automatically in any original work once it is fixed in a tangible medium. **You don't have to do anything to copyright your work.** Certainly, there are benefits to providing notice that the work is copyrighted, so it's good to make use of that © symbol just to let people know, "hey, this is mine."

However, placing a copyright notice on a work is not a substitute for registration. A copyright owner can take steps to enhance the protections of their copyright, and the most important of those is registering the work.

US COPYRIGHT OFFICE

Copyrights are registered with the US Copyright Office, located in the Library of Congress in Washington, D.C. The Office was established in 1790, and has been part of the Library of Congress since 1870.[285] Since its founding, the Copyright Office has registered more than 33,654,000 copyrights.[286] In a single

---

[285] US Copyright Office, "Overview" https://www.copyright.gov/about/
[286] *Id.*

year[287], the Copyright Office registered more than 443,000 copyrights, collected over $33 million in registration fees, and forwarded 552,000 submitted works, with a value of $45.2 million, for archiving in the Library of Congress.[288]

The Librarian of Congress appoints the Register of Copyrights (who is also the Director of the US Copyright Office)[289]. The Register serves a ten-year term, and heads an office of around 440 people.[290]

REGISTRATION: MAKING IT OFFICIAL

I said it before, and I'll say it here again: There is no such thing as a "poor man's copyright." There's a popular myth that if you make a copy of your work, put it in an envelope, and mail it to yourself, the postmark will be legal proof of your copyright. The fact is, that's nonsense.[291] Copyright exists just by the act of you creating a copyrightable work. You don't have to mail things to yourself, you don't have to do a special dance in the moonlight, you don't need to need to do anything: you have a copyright.

What you *don't* have, though, is a work that's protected by the law, and the right to sue an infringer in court and collect statutory damages. The only way to get that is to register your copyright.

Let's be clear. You are not required to register a copyright, but doing so will ensure that your claim is valid and enforceable. With an unregistered copyright, you can send cease and desist

---

[287] 2020
[288] US Copyright Office, "Overview"
https://www.copyright.gov/about/small-claims/
[289] In 2017, legislation was introduced to make the Register of Copyrights a presidential appointment, but the bill failed to pass.
[290] The current Register of Copyrights is Shira Perlmutter, who was appointed in October 2020.
[291] https://www.copyright.gov/help/faq/faq-general.html

letters and hire a lawyer to send threatening memos to the infringer, but that's about it.

Title 17 U. S. C. §411(a) says "no civil action for infringement of the copyright in any United States work shall be instituted until preregistration or registration of the copyright claim has been made in accordance with this title."[292] That means a copyright holder can't sue an infringer unless the copyright is registered, or at least until the work has been submitted to the Copyright Office for registration.[293] But a recent Supreme Court decision changed that a little.

In 2019, the Supreme Court unanimously held that although the creator of a work holds the full bundle of copyright sticks from the moment a work is created, the creator can't file a lawsuit for infringement until <u>after</u> their copyright registration application has been approved by the Copyright Office.[294]

Registration means that in a copyright infringement lawsuit, the court will accept the validity of your copyright right off the bat[295], without you having to prove anything other than the fact that it's registered. It also means that you are entitled to collect damages established by law: a minimum of *$750 per work infringed*, and a maximum of *$30,000 per work infringed*.[296] If the infringement was found to be intentional and not just accidental, the statutory maximum is $150,000.[297] Statutory damages also include attorneys' fees and court costs.

---

[292] Title 17 USC §411(a). But see *Fourth Estate Public Benefit Corp. v Wall-Street.com*, LLC, 139 S.Ct. 881 (2019)

[293] *Id.* Notice of the lawsuit and a copy of the complaint must be given to the Register of Copyrights before the lawsuit is begun.

[294] *Fourth Estate Public Benefit Corp. v Wall-Street.com*, LLC, 139 S.Ct. 881 (2019)

[295] The fancy lawyer way of saying this is that registration is *prima facie* evidence of your copyright's validity.

[296] 17 USC § 504(c)(1)

[297] 17 USC § 504(c)(2)

So there's a good reason to register. Also, registration is easy: Registering your copyright involves filling out an online form, paying a fee[298], and waiting two to six months for the Copyright Office to review and approve your application.

The most common online application fee is $65 ($45 for single author, single work, not a work for hire, submitted online). The fee schedule actually goes as high as $500 depending on the type of work and the complexity of the approval process. For instance, registration of a "vessel design"—such as a boat—is $500; collections of written, unpublished, photographic, or musical works is $55 to $85; more than two issues of a serial is $35. Fees for mailed, paper applications are higher, so use the online registration system if you can.[299]

A certificate of registration creates a public record of key facts relating to the authorship and ownership of the work, including

- title of the work
- author
- name and address of the copyright owner
- year of creation
- information about whether the work is published, has been previously registered, or includes preexisting material.

Let's take a closer look at the statutory penalties for infringement, which are found in the United States Code.

17 USC§ 501 Copyright Infringement

Anyone who violates a copyright owner's exclusive rights (that is, anyone who steals your sticks) is subject to the following penalties:

---

[298] US Copyright Office, *Circular 4*: Copyright Office Fees (rev'd 2021)
[299] Check current fees at www.copyright.gov/ about/fees.html.

1. **Injunctions**—that is, they have to stop infringing.

2. **Seizure and destruction** of all infringing copies made in violation of the copyright owner's rights along with anything used to produce it, any digital files related to it, and any business records regarding it.

3. **Payment** of costs and attorney's fees.[300] and either:

    a. **Actual damages** suffered by the copyright owner as a result of the infringement, plus any profits infringer made from the infringement, or

    b. **Statutory damages** in the amount of not less than $750 or more than $30,000 as the court deems just. If the court finds that the infringement was intentional, the judge may increase the statutory damages to as much as $150,000.

©ASE STUDY In 2008, the US Postal Service began to work on designing a new Forever Stamp—the kind with no price on them, that are good even if the postage rate goes up.[301]

The Post Office decided that a picture of the Statute of Liberty would be good, so they got access to several photo repositories, such as Getty Images and Shutterstock, to look for images of the Statue of Liberty's face. The manager of stamp development began the search for a new image, sorting through the repositories and picking out the ones he liked. The Post Office paid Getty Images $1500 for a license to use the image he finally picked. The Post Office proceeded to print and distribute 10.5 billion copies of the stamp, of which 4.9 billion were sold, amounting to $2.1 billion dollars in revenue to the USPS.

---

[301] *Davidson v USPS*, United States Court of Federal Claims, No. 13-942C (2018)

Robert Davidson is a professional sculptor. Among his works is the Statute of Liberty replica on display outside the New York New York casino in Las Vegas. As luck would have it, the image selected by the USPS was *not* the famous Statue of Liberty in Upper New York Bay, but a photo of its one-half scale replica on the Las Vegas Strip. The USPS had paid Getty Images for the photo, but Getty did not own the rights to the *subject* of the photo, which was not the Statue of Liberty—which as a federal monument is in the public domain—but rather a Statute of Liberty-like sculpture, that actually depicted the artist's mother-in-law as the famous Lady Liberty.

New York-New York. Las Vegas. (24321302428).jpg by Bernard Spragg (Creative Commons CC0 1.0 Universal Public Domain Dedication), modified

In awarding actual damages to the sculptor, the court considered a number of factors. The court looked at expert testimony from agents who negotiate licenses with government agencies, and determined that if the USPS followed its own practices, it should have paid a 5% royalty to Davidson. 4,948,761,166 Liberty stamps were sold. The total amount collected for those sales was $2,190,414,155. USPS also sold about $30,000 worth of collector items (coffee cups, t-shirts, etc.) with the image on them. Taking 5% of all that generated $3,554,946.54 in damages due to the sculptor.

And that will buy a lot of stamps.

Copyright Small Claims

In 2019, Congress passed the Copyright Alternative in Small-Claims Enforcement Act or the CASE Act. CASE established a Copyright Claims Board (CCB) within the US Copyright Office, which acts like an optional, "quick and easy" small claims court for copyright lawsuits.[302] The filing fee for a CCB case is only $50, about an eighth of the normal fee for filing in federal court. Parties represent themselves, and proceedings are carried out remotely.

There are three key things to keep in mind about CCB claims:

1. Normal copyright claims require that the Copyright Office has approved an application. CCB cases only require that the copyright holder has submitted the registration materials and fees to the Copyright Office.
2. Damages in CCB lawsuits cannot exceed $30,000 *per case*. Claims made outside CCB can be anywhere from $30,000 to $150,000 *per work* for statutory damages, and virtually unlimited for actual damages.
3. CCB is empowered to hear not just infringement cases brought by copyright holders, but suits brought by third parties (for instance, a maker of TikToks or reaction videos on YouTube) for wrongful takedowns of their content. CCB can also provide third-party users with an opinion about whether or not their proposed use is a fair use.

Criminal Copyright Offenses

Some types of copyright infringements are actually federal *criminal* offenses. The statute that outlines the criminal elements of infringement is located in the criminal code in a chapter called "Stolen Property"—which makes sense, since

---

[302] 86 FR 21990, "Copyright Alternative in Small-Claims Enforcement ("CASE") Act Regulations: Expedited Registration and FOIA" (2021); https://www.copyright.gov/about/small-claims/

copyright infringement is in fact a theft of intellectual property.[303] Criminal copyright infringement is prosecuted by the Department of Justice. That means that people can (and do) pay large fines or even go to prison for copyright infringement.

Criminal copyright offenses typically include things like

- Making a video recording of a movie playing in a theater;[304]
- Distributing pirated music or movies;[305]
- Bypassing anti-copying measures;
- Setting up an online, subscription-based service that allowed users to stream and download copyrighted TV programs without the permission of the copyright owners;[306] and
- Operating an illegal music streaming service.[307]

The penalty statutes distinguish between infringement for profit and infringement motivated by other, non-financial gain factors. That's important: someone can commit a federal copyright crime and go to prison even if they're not doing the infringing for money.[308]

To qualify as a criminal offense, the infringement must be intentional, and must meet specific value, quantity, and timing requirements. The infringement may be classified as a felony or misdemeanor.[309]

---

[303] 18 USC § 2319
[304] *US v Logan*, Case 1:08-cr-00217-RWR (DC, 2008)
[305] *US v Shabazz*, 724 F.2d 1536 (11th Cir. 1984)
[306] https://www.justice.gov/usao-edva/pr/eight-defendants-charged-running-two-largest-illegal-streaming-services-us
[307] https://www.justice.gov/usao-ndga/pr/owner-sharebeastcom-sentenced-copyright-infringement
[308] 17 USC § 506(a)(1)(B)
[309] If 10 or more copies are made of a copyrighted work with a value greater than $2500, the infringement is a felony. If less than ten and less than $2500, it's a misdemeanor.

For willful infringement with or without a profit motive, the law establishes fines ranging from $100,000 to $250,000 ($500,000 for corporations), and prison terms between one and ten years.[310] Fines are the same in cases of willful infringement without profit motive, but the prison terms range from one to six years.[311] In both for-profit and not-for-profit cases, the law also requires restitution to the copyright holder—that is, actual damages.[312]

And now that we know what the stakes are for registering your copyright (lawsuits, damages, and potentially sending the rascal to prison), let's look at the mechanics of registering your copyright.

REGISTRATION PROCESS

An application for copyright registration contains three essential elements:

1. a completed application form,
2. a nonrefundable filing fee, and
3. a copy of the work being registered

There are two ways to apply for copyright registration: online and with paper forms. Online registration through the electronic Copyright Office at https://www.copyright.gov/registration is the preferred way to register your work. However, if you prefer to file hard copies through the mail, you can download the necessary forms from https://www.copyright.gov/forms.

There are several advantages to online filing, however:

---

[310] 17 USC § 506(a)(1)(A); 18 USC § 2319(b)
[311] *Id.*
[312] *Id.*

- Discounted filing fee ($45[313] rather than $125 for paper filing)[314]
- Faster processing time (an average of 1.6 months for online submissions, versus 9.5 months for an average paper submission)[315]
- Ability to track your registration's progress online
- Secure payment by credit or debit card (paper submission require a check or money order)

When you receive your registration certificate from the Copyright Office, you'll see that the effective date of your copyright registration is the date the Office received all the required parts of your submission—the application, filing fee, and deposit of a copy of the work.

You do not have to wait to receive your certificate before you publish or produce your work or place a copyright notice on it. The only timing limitation is that you can't file an infringement lawsuit until the Copyright Office has started processing your application. If your application was not accepted, you'll get an explanation of the decision from the Copyright Office, and the decision can be appealed.[316]

Requirements for a Deposit Copy

The general rule is that applicants must deposit two complete copies of the best edition within 3 months after a work is published (authors of unpublished works only need to submit

---

[313] For a single filer, one work, one author, not made for hire; all other filings are $65.
[314] Filing fees are current as of publication, but may change. See 37 CFR §201.3 for updates.
[315] US Copyright Office, *Circular 4*: Copyright Office Fees (2021)
[316] The current fee for filing an appeal is $350. US Copyright Office *Compendium*: Chapter 1700 Administrative Appeals (rev'd 2022)

one copy). Works that are available in both print and electronic formats may be submitted in their digital form.[317]

Copies of all works under copyright protection that have been published or distributed in the United States must be deposited with the Copyright Office within 3 months of the date of first publication.[318] The copies will be used by the Copyright Office in evaluating your registration application, and will be archived in the Library of Congress after approval.[319] Obviously, that's easier with some types of works (literary or musical scores for instance) than others (sculptural or architectural works could be cumbersome to email to the Copyright Office).

Alternatives to the General Rule

The Copyright Office accepts a range of types of deposits, depending on the type of work. Remember, though, that two copies of a published work is the norm, or one copy of an unpublished work. The following are some examples of alternative submissions.

Architecture

Submit one complete copy of an architectural drawing or blueprint in visually perceptible form showing exterior elevations when viewed from the front, rear, sides, and top down, and any interior spaces or structural design elements for which you're claiming copyright. When you provide the date and place of first publication, remember that an architectural work is considered "published" when its plans or drawings are distributed or made available to the public--construction of a building is not considered publication.[320]

---

[317] US Copyright Office, *Compendium*, Chapter 1500: Deposits, § 1507.1 (rev'd 2021)

[318] US Copyright Office, *Circular 7D*: Mandatory Deposit of Copies or Phonorecords (rev'd 2010)

[319] 17 USC § 407

[320] 37 CFR § 202.11(c)(5)

Audiovisual Works

Audiovisual works can be submitted on CD-ROM, or if not available on CD-ROM, then by a videotape or a series of photographs showing representative portions of the work, along with a written description and synopsis of the work.[321]

T-Shirts, Art Prints, and Reproductions

The Copyright Office prefers that you provide a *physical copy* of a T-shirt imprint, art prints, and other reproductions if they can be folded to 4" thickness or less. If the item can't be folded to 4" thickness or less, then photographs of the imprint or reproduction are allowed.[322]

If you intend to submit a photograph as the identifying material for the claim, be sure that you don't refer to the reproduction as a "photograph." If you say "photograph" in the application, the Copyright Office may mistakenly assume that you intend to register authorship of a photo of the item, not the item itself.

Cartoons, Comic Strips, and Comic Books You should be careful when claiming a copyright for a character—as discussed in an earlier chapter, while characters can be copyrighted, there are special considerations to keep in mind.

Choreographic Works You don't have to dance your dance in DC. Acceptable forms of deposit include dance notation, written descriptions, videos, illustrations, drawings, and photographs.[323]

---

[321] US Copyright Office, *Compendium*, Chapter 1500: Deposits, 1509.2(E)(2) (rev'd 2021).
[322] US Copyright Office, *Circular 40a*: Deposit Requirements for Visual Arts Works (rev'd 2015).
[323] US Copyright Office, *Compendium*, Chapter 1500: Deposits, § 1509.2(D) (rev'd 2021). See also, Chapter 800: Works of the Performing Arts, §§ 805.3(D) and 806.3(D).

Computer Games & Programs

Submit the source code for the specific version of the computer program you want to register. You can submit the entire source code for the program, or you can submit a representative portion. It's sufficient to submit one copy of the first twenty-five pages and last twenty-five pages of the source code. If the entire program is less than fifty pages, submit the entire source code (be sure to notify the Copyright Office that you're submitting the entire code. [CIRCULAR 61]

If your program is on a CD-ROM, which is still preferred, then the Copyright Office requires that you submit "one complete copy of the entire CD-ROM package, including a complete copy of any accompanying operating software and instructional manual."[324]

Equivalent units For a program that is not represented by "pages," you can submit whatever the page equivalent is. For instance, 40 lines of code is generally considered equal to a page. So for a non-paginated program, the first and last thousand lines of code would be considered an acceptably complete copy.[325]

Fabric Designs

For original artwork in fabric, wallpaper, carpeting, floor tile, or even wrapping paper, or other similar sheet-like materials, submit one complete copy in the form of an actual swatch or piece of the material large enough to show all elements of the work in which copyright is claimed, and the degree to which they repeat.[326]

---

[324] 37 CFR § 202.20(c)(2)(xix)(A). See also, *Compendium* Chapter 1500: Deposits, § 1509.1(F)(5)
[325] https://www.copyright.gov/eco/help-deposit.html
[326] US Copyright Office, *Compendium*, Chapter 1500: Deposits, § 1509.3(F) (rev'd 2021)

Games (Tabletop)

One physical copy if the container is no larger than 12" x 24" x 6"; otherwise written descriptions and photographs are allowed.[327]

Jewelry

A physical sample if the work is no larger than 4" x 4" x 4"; otherwise written descriptions, drawings, and photographs are permitted.[328] Because a registration only covers the copyrightable authorship that is clearly shown in the application, be sure to submit images of the jewelry from multiple angles: front, back, top-down, bottom, and side views.[329]

Literary Works

The Copyright Office defines a "literary work" as "a nondramatic work that explains, describes, or narrates a particular subject, theme, or idea through the use of narrative, descriptive, or explanatory text, rather than dialog or dramatic action."[330] Think of literary works as things that are meant to be read, rather than performed.

These works include fiction, nonfiction, poetry, directories and catalogs, textbooks, reference works, advertising copy, computer programs*, videogames*, databases*, serials, book jackets, instructional works, and compilations.[331]

---

[327] US Copyright Office, *Circular 40a*: Deposit Requirements for Visual Arts Works §§ 1509.3(F), 1509.1(E) (rev'd 2015)
[328] US Copyright Office, *Compendium*, Chapter 1500: Deposits, § 1509.3(C) (rev'd 2021)
[329] *Id.*
[330] US Copyright Office, *Circular 40a*: Deposit Requirements for Visual Arts Works § 1509.1 (rev'd 2015)
[331] *Id.*, see also 37 CFR § 202.3(b)(1)(i)
* See Computer Games & Programs above for specific submission information

For any published literary work, you should submit two copies in a digital format (if available), or in print. For unpublished literary works, a single copy is sufficient.[332]

Published collections of poetry (as well as other collected works) may be registered on a single form with a single fee if all the poems are owned by the same copyright claimant, and are all in the same medium.[333]

Movies

Submit one complete copy of the published or unpublished movie, along with a written description of its content or a synopsis of its plot.[334] The Copyright Office defines a "complete copy" of a movie as being when all visual and audio elements are final, and "clean, undamaged, undeteriorated, and free of splices, and …defects that would interfere with the performance of the work or that would cause mechanical, visual, or audible defects or distortions."[335]

Oversized Works

Any work that is more than 96" in any dimension is considered "oversized" by the Copyright Office. You can submit drawings, photographs, or other physical renderings of the oversized work instead of a physical copy.[336]

Sound Recordings

Submit two phonorecords of the sound recording, along with copies of any associated material you want to protect, such as liner notes, cover images, etc.

---

[332] *Id.*
[333] https://www.copyright.gov/register/tx-poetry.html
[334] US Copyright Office, *Compendium*, Chapter 1500: Deposits, § 1509.2(F) (rev'd 2021). See also, 37 CFR § 202.20(c)(2)(ii)
[335] 37 CFR § 202.20(b)(2)(vii).
[336] *Id.*, § 1506

Three-Dimensional Works: Sculptures, Toys, Dolls, Molds, Relief Plaques, Statues, Etc.

Where the actual work is too large to submit, you can submit photographs, drawings, written descriptions, and videos of the work. As with other such submissions, be sure to be clear that you're submitting the work depicted in the drawing, photo, or video, and not the drawing, photo, or video itself.

Don't worry: if you make a good-faith mistake in your registration, it won't invalidate your copyright. The US Supreme Court recently decided that a copyright registration that includes an error or inaccuracy is still valid, if the person registering made a mistake of law or didn't know there was an error.[337]

THE FINAL DECISION: REGISTER OR NOT?

It's clear there are lots of advantages to registering your copyright, so why not just do it? Well, there are a few things to consider that aren't really "disadvantages" to registration, but more like reality-check factors.

Let's do a quick list of pros and cons:

PRO	CON
Public record of your copyright	Expense
Right to sue for infringement	Infringement unlikely
Statutory damages	Revisions

On the "pro" side—which we've covered a lot here and in other chapters—registration creates a public record of your copyright, which can be used as *prima facie* evidence of its existence in the event of an infringement suit—"prima facie" is a fancy lawyer way of saying the court will automatically accept the existence of your copyright "on its face," without needing any other proof.

---

[337] *Unicolors, Inc. v. H&M Hennes & Mauritz, L.P.*, No. 20-915 (2022)

An infringement lawsuit is also on the pro side, since only registered copyrights are protectable by legal action. And if you do sue for infringement, you have statutory damages available as an option, if your actual damages from the infringement are really sort of small.

On the "con" side, though, are some things to think about. First, while registration is not wildly expensive, money is money, and if you don't *have* to spend it, then why spend it? Second, ask yourself how likely it is that anyone is going to infringe your work. If you don't think it's likely—either because your work is unique to you, or because it's never going to be seen by a big audience of potential copiers, or for whatever reason, then maybe you want to rely on your "automatic" copyright—the way anything is copyrighted by its creator when it's created—and send threatening letters written by your cousin the lawyer.

Finally, remember that copyright registrations are for the final versions of a work. If you plan on doing updates, revisions, or modifications to your work over time, you'll need to re-register.

There's a safety net for you, too: Courts have consistently held that the holder of an unregistered copyright who learns of an infringement can go ahead and register their work in order to sue. So the good news is that if you've chosen not to register and someone copies your work, you still have the option of registering and suing.

Remember that a copyright infringement suit cannot be filed when you submit your registration. It can only be filed <u>after</u> a copyright has been successfully registered—a process that can take from two to ten months. [338]

The value that anyone puts on any of these pro or con factors will be different, depending on their own priorities and the nature of the work itself. It's certainly not the biggest decision

---

[338] *Fourth Estate Public Benefit Corp. v. Wall-Street.com*, 586 US ___ (2019),

anyone will ever be faced with, but while you probably should register your copyright, it may make sense for you to not bother.

 **So what do you take away from all this? Here are four key points to remember:**

1. You don't *have* to register your copyright: it exists from the moment you create something in tangible form...
2. ...But if you want to sue someone for infringing your copyright, and to collect actual or statutory damages, you *must* register it with the US Copyright Office.
3. The Copyright Office prefers the best available actual copy of a work, but will accept photographs, drawing, and written descriptions under some circumstances, such as a large work or a computer program.
4. Decide for yourself whether or not registration is right for you and your work.

Chapter 14

Open Access

This book is absolutely about copyright, and how you can protect your creative works from being used or modified or distributed by other people without your permission.

But sometimes, creators decide that they would prefer to have the widest possible exposure of their work, regardless of their bundle of sticks. However, they don't want to just throw away their creative work. **Open Access** is an alternative model to traditional copyright that tries to balance the rights of creators with ensuring that their works are exposed to the world and freely used by others.

Open Access (OA) is mostly concerned with publications. Although its origins lie in scientific and technical research publishing; OA isn't just about books and articles and poems and stuff, although that's where most of the action is. It's also about graphic art, photography, and other creative works as well—essentially anything that can be copyrighted can be OA. Sites like Wikimedia Commons provide free public access to original graphic art and photography works by creators who've donated their content so that others can freely use it.[339]

TRADITIONAL PUBLISHING

Over 30 years in the publishing industry has made me more than aware that the relationship between an author and a publisher can be a tricky one.

At its best, it's a partnership: The "ideas person" and the "production person" get together and accomplish the mutually beneficial goal of disseminating the author's work to as wide an audience as possible.

Ideally, the publisher-author relationship is a well-intentioned effort to recognize the value that each partner brings to the publishing effort. The author typically provides his or her research, analysis, observations, opinions, resources, and conclusions in a form that we'd all generally recognize. That's obviously the core component of the value of any work: the work itself. That's the thing the author is an expert in.

The publisher provides other stuff, because the publisher is not a subject matter expert. The publisher is presumably an expert in what content people want to buy, and how to get that content into buyers' hands. Publishers also bring editorial, production, distribution, and marketing services to the table.

The publisher provides a tidying of the author's language, for instance, so that their particular weaknesses with grammar and punctuation don't get in the way of what they're trying to say. The publisher provides the visual context for the work: decisions on the cover design, how to best display the author's

---

[339] The photograph of the Statue of Liberty replica in front of the New York New York casino in Las Vegas in Chapter 13 was found in the Wikimedia Commons database, where the photographer posted it copyright-free.

graphics, what other graphic elements to include, how to make the book more accessible and more marketable.

The publisher assumes all the functions of printing, marketing, promoting, selling, and fulfilling sales. New publishing technologies also give publishers additional value-adding ways to present the work, as well as ways to link the work to others like it (or to works that cite it or that it cites).

The challenge is that this relationship works optimally in a tightly controlled supply environment: that is, in a print-based world in which publishers print books (or magazines or periodicals or whatever) and people buy them.

That's increasingly not the world we live in.

The traditional view of the publishing world is not entirely relevant today, because we're no longer living in an exclusively print publishing world. Access to what was once the publisher's primary service—distribution—is now pretty much in the hands of anyone who has access to the Internet. The result is that many authors have decided that the old measure of a work's value—its financial return to the author and publisher—is no longer relevant.

For some authors, that means they're more comfortable self-publishing their works, taking on what was once the publisher's exclusive burden of production, marketing, and sales. Amazon's bookstore, for instance, has no shortage of author-published works—like the one you're reading, for example.[340]

---

[340] My literary agent shopped this book to literally dozens of publishers, all of whom praised its relevance and potential interest to a lot of people—but not enough people. It was universally found to be too "niche" to guarantee publishers a reasonable return on their editorial, production, and marketing investment. Fair enough; but my costs are much lower, and Amazon is a terrific publishing partner, as some of my friends have found. And thank you for reading this book!

Amazon and other sites can provide a one-stop layout, printing, sales, and fulfilment platform, charging a royalty on sales to pay for the service, and flipping the usual publisher-author model in which the author is compensated by a percentage of sales. Other authors prefer to promote their works offline, at conventions, classes, events, and bookstores. The reward for self-publishing is that the author gets to keep all the revenue, not just their 15% royalty. Of course, the authors are also taking on all the risks, the expenses, and the workload themselves as well.

OPEN ACCESS

For some content creators, self-publishing is not the answer if it continues to hide their work behind a shield of copyright. Those authors and content creators believe that information wants to be free, and post their work on the Web for others to freely enjoy...and also to publish, adapt, perform, display, and reproduce.

The Dawn of Open Access

The Open Access movement began in the 1990s as the Internet enabled wider—and generally free—access to content. Initially, open access was focused on scholarly and scientific research.

Under the mantra, "information wants to be free," OA advocates pressured universities, institutional publishers, and commercial publishers of scientific research, to make publicly-funded research (which most scientific research is, at least in part) freely available to the public. Their goal was ultimately to dismantle the traditional scholarly publishing industry and replace it with digital content curated by volunteers and hosted on freely-accessible server space donated by university libraries and other nonprofits.

The tradition of scholars publishing their research work in journals—usually without payment and without retaining copyright—could be combined with the Internet to ensure that anyone, anywhere, anytime could immediately and freely access the results of scholarly research online.

The first online repository for scientific papers was created in 1991 in Los Alamos, New Mexico. Today, arXiv, as it's known, contains over two million scholarly articles in the fields of physics, mathematics, computer science, quantitative biology, quantitative finance, statistics, electrical engineering and systems science, and economics.[341] In 2000, BioMed Central and PubMed Central, free digital archives for biomedical and life sciences publications, started making more free content available to researchers.[342] In 2008, the huge multinational publisher Springer purchased BioMed Central, embracing the open access challenge and ensuring that OA was mainstream.

CREATIVE COMMONS

Creative Commons is a nonprofit, volunteer-run organization founded in 2001 by Harvard Law Professor Lawrence Lessig and the Center for the Study of the Public Domain at Duke Law School.[343] Creative Commons developed a standardized licensing system to give authors control over how freely their work could be shared. Currently, over 2 billion creative works carry a Creative Commons license.[344]

Creative Commons engages in a wide range of activities designed to promote OA. Primarily, Creative Commons manages and evolves its licensing model, a standardized permissions system that lets authors and creators retain credit and some control over their work, while still making it freely available.[345] The organization also lobbies and encourages institutions and

---

[341] https://arxiv.org/stats/monthly_submissions
[342] https://www.biomedcentral.com/
[343] https://creativecommons.org/about/
[344] https://creativecommons.org/
[345] *Id.*

governments adopt and enforce OA principles and Creative Commons licensing

Creative Commons License

So what exactly is a Creative Commons license, and what does it do?

A Creative Commons license is "a standardized way to grant the public permission to use their creative work under copyright law....[T]he presence of a Creative Commons license on a copyrighted work answers the question, 'What can I do with this work?'"[346]

The license itself:

- Allows creators to retain copyright while permitting others to copy, distribute, and make some more or less limited uses of their work;
- Ensures that creators get credit for their work; and
- Requires licensees to get permission to do any of the things with a work the license doesn't clearly allow. Licensees must also credit the creator, keep copyright notices intact on all copies of the work, and link to the Creative Commons license from copies of the work.[347]

Creative Commons licenses are recognized and accepted internationally, and last as long as copyright lasts. The difference is that creators can choose to grant permissions and retain certain rights on a global scale, rather than doing one-off license agreements.

There are six types of Creative Commons license. From least to most restrictive they are:

---

[346] https://creativecommons.org/about/cclicenses/
[347] https://creativecommons.org/licenses/

CC 0

The CC 0 (zero) license is the most pure expression of OA. A creator who registers their work with a CC 0 license is basically placing the work in the public domain, with no restriction whatsoever.

CC BY

CC BY is an attribution license that lets others distribute, remix, tweak, change, and build on your work, even commercially, as long as they credit you for the original creation and specify what changes they made. This is the broadest, most liberal Creative Commons license, and certainly ensures the greatest possible distribution and use of licensed materials. The "BY" means that the original creators must be credited, because the work is *BY* them.

CC BY-SA

Also known as "Share Alike," CC BY-SA is a slightly more restrictive license than CC BY—but only slightly. Under this license, anyone may remix, tweak, and build on your work even for commercial purposes, as long as they credit you, specify the changes, and license their new creations under the same terms as your license. That is, if you have a CC BY-SA license on your work, someone else can use it to create something new, but their new work must be distributed under a CC BY-SA license. They can't use your work and then put a full no-license copyright lid on it, and they can't make it public domain through a CC 0. In a CC BY-SA license, the "SA" stands for "share-alike," which is what people have to do with their new work.

The logic behind having a "Share Alike" license is pretty obvious. A creator who made something original and then decides to share it with the world under a Creative Commons license is giving up some control of the work and some potential revenue streams. Without the SA license, other people could use that original content to generate revenue for themselves, and hold on to total control of the derivative work based on the original creator's efforts. And that's just not fair—a good act of sharing shouldn't be punished.

CC BY-ND

The CC BY-ND is a little more restrictive than SA. Under BY-ND, third parties are allowed to redistribute the content, commercially or non-commercially, as long as they credit the original creator (BY) and as long as there are no changes to the original content. The ND stands for "No Derivatives" because the license doesn't allow derivative uses. That means your work can be freely distributed, but only as-is.

CC BY-NC

The CC BY-NC permits others to use your work, including making changes or derivative works. The limitations here are that the original creator must be credited (BY) and any use of the work must be non-commercial. That means users don't have the right to make money from your open access work. On the other hand, they are permitted to create derivative works (unlike ND) and apply a different Creative Commons license from the one you used (unlike SA)—or not apply a license at all.

CC BY-NC-SA

The CC BY-NC-SA license is basically a combination of three less-restrictive licenses. Under this license, others can use and change your work, but only for non-commercial purposes, only if they credit you, and only if their new derivative work is licensed under a BY-NC-SA license too.

CC BY-NC-ND

Finally, the CC BY-NC-ND license is perhaps the most restrictive of the Creative Commons licenses. Under this license, users can essentially share your work with others as long as they credit you, but they can't change it in any way and any use must be non-commercial. If you're interested in maintaining the "purity" of your original work, but maybe in sharing it for educational purposes, this would be the license that accomplishes that goal.

COPYRIGHT AND CREATIVE COMMONS

It's important to note that the Creative Commons licenses do not replace copyright law. In fact, they operate comfortably within current copyright law. As we discussed back in Chapter 1, the copyright holder has a bundle of rights and can choose to share them with others or not, through licenses. The Creative Commons licenses are simply a uniform, standardized, generally-recognized way to license your content to anyone in the world who might be interested in using it, without having to create dozens or hundreds of individual license agreements. Creative Commons' goal is to create a world "beyond all rights reserved."[348]

So here's how it works:

1. You create your content, and by creating it copyright automatically exists for you.
2. But you want to be sure you can successfully protect your bundle of sticks, so you register your copyright with the US Copyright Office.
3. Now you want your work to be useful to others, so you decide to use a Creative Commons license.
4. Go to https://creativecommons.org/choose and answer a few simple questions on the Creative Commons site. The tool will recommend which of the licenses is best suited to what you want to do, and will auto-generate the html code you can apply to your work on your webpage.
5. You can apply the same or different licenses to all the works on your site. You can also provide specific

---

[348] https://creativecommons.org/licenses/by-nc-sa/4.0/

instructions for how you want to be credited. The license you've selected will appear on your webpage looking something like this one, which applies to one of my photographs:

In this example, there are three active links in this license statement on the work. The first is the title of the work, which links to the site where it was originally posted. The second is the name of the creator, for purposes of attribution. The third link describes the type of license granted, and links to the Creative Commons site's definition of the type of license you've chosen:

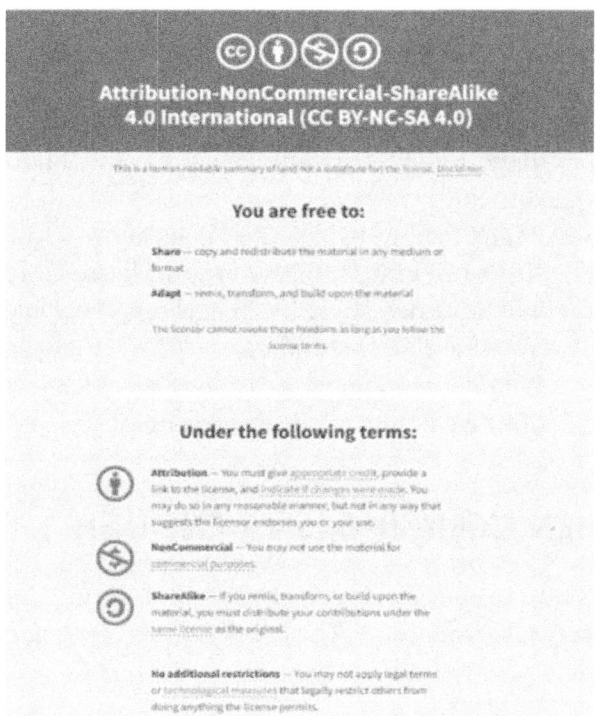

You can also post your work on sites that support open access and Creative Commons licenses, like Flickr, WordPress, Wikimedia Commons, Wikipedia, YouTube, Etsy, Pinterest, Freesound, and Vimeo. However, just because the sites support Creative Commons doesn't mean that the content posted there is automatically under a license for use: you'll need to inspect the work and its information closely to ensure you're using work that's under a Creative Commons license.

> *Remember that just because you license your work doesn't mean you lose those rights yourself. You can also do all the things you give others permission to do, unless you specify that your license is an exclusive grant of rights.*

How to Find Licensed Works

So you're a creative person, and you want to use some images or other content to create something new. It's surprisingly easy to find works that are available under Creative Commons licenses on the Internet.

- Creative Commons offers a search engine on its site dedicated to crawling the Web and finding licensed content.[349]
- Repository websites like Flickr allow you to narrow a site-wide search by the type of license the content is under. Other sites, like Pexels, or Pixabay, offer only freely-usable content.
- Wikimedia Commons is exclusively a repository of Creative Commons licensed content.

WHEN LICENSING ISN'T ENOUGH

For some OA purists, much of what Creative Commons does is unacceptably moderate. The Free Cultural Works movement (or

---

[349] https://wordpress.org/openverse/

Free Culture Movement) shares its roots with Creative Commons, but takes the idea of open access much more literally. The goal of the Free Culture Movement is to eliminate the current copyright-focused culture, in which uses by anyone other than the copyright holder require explicit permission (what the movement refers to as "permission culture"). Instead, the Free Culture Movement wants to replace permission culture with a "free culture" in which the free and open distribution, modification, adaptation and derivative use of creative work is encouraged and celebrated.

> The free-culture movement is a social movement that promotes the freedom to distribute and modify the creative works of others in the form of free content or open content without compensation to, or the consent of, the work's original creators, by using the Internet and other forms of media.[350]

While Creative Commons has established an ecosystem of licenses that operates within traditional copyright, the Free Culture Movement finds such restrictions only marginally tolerable, preferring complete, unlimited access to works.[351]

While rejecting traditional copyright as overly restrictive, most proponents of the Free Culture Movement allow for some limitations, however, such as requiring attribution of the creator of the original work.[352] That's why there can be overlap between the goals of the Free Culture Movement and Creative Commons: The CC: BY, and CC: SA licenses are both considered acceptably "free" for example, because they only protect accreditation and openness. The CC 0 license is the most acceptable, because it is in fact totally free of any restriction. Other Creative Commons licenses are considered too restrictive to be considered "free content."

---

[350] https://www.wikiwand.com/en/Free-culture_movement
[351] https://freedomdefined.org/Definition
[352] *Id.*

CHOICES

Depending on how interested you are in protecting your legal rights as a creator, then, you have choices:

- You can use the existing copyright structure and allow others to use your works only if you specifically license them to do so; or
- You can use Creative Commons licenses to grant general permission for certain uses, with specific restrictions; or
- You can embrace the Free Culture Movement and grant the world unlimited license to do whatever they like with your work.

In the end, it's all up to you.

 **So what do you take away from all this? Here are four key points to remember:**

1. Traditional publishing offers many benefits to authors, but there are downsides as well.
2. Copyright law is by its nature restrictive; the goal of the open access movement is to leverage technology to make creativity, art, and information more widely accessible, and to create a society in which re-use, re-purposing, and derivative use are not just permitted, but encouraged.
3. Creative Commons licenses give creators the power to easily make their works widely available but with a variety of customizable restrictions.
4. The Free Culture Movement generally rejects the limitations of copyright, and Creative Commons licenses, in favor of establishing a culture in which free access to, and use of, other peoples' creative work is unrestricted.

Chapter 15
A Bit About Trademarks

Throughout this book's chapters on copyright, I've frequently said something like "copyright won't protect this, but you might consider trademark as an alternative." That's what this chapter is about: trademarking as an alternative way to protect your creative work. In this chapter, we'll introduce the fundamental principles of trademark law, specifically the role of trademarks as intellectual property. Consider this your foot in the door of trademarking.

Copyright and trademark are not mutually exclusive, and are frequently used together to ensure the protection of content creators' rights. "Harry Potter," for example, is copyrighted as the name of a character in a series of copyrighted books by J.K. Rowling, but it's also trademarked by both Rowling and the movie studio that produced the Harry Potter films.

WHAT IS A TRADEMARK?

A trademark is generally a word, phrase, symbol, design, or a combination of those elements, that identifies and distinguishes the goods of one party from those of others.[353]

---

[353] https://www.uspto.gov/trademarks/basics/what-trademark

It's governed in the US by the Trademark Act of 1946, generally known as "the Lanham Act." The Lanham Act says:

> "The term "**trademark**" includes any word, name, symbol, or device, or any combination thereof—
>
> (1) used by a person, or
>
> (2) which a person has a bona fide intention to use in commerce ... to identify and distinguish his or her goods, including a **unique product**, from those manufactured or sold by others ...."[354]

(And keep in mind that the word *person* legally includes corporations.)

TM and R

You're probably familiar with the *R* and *TM* symbols. Like the C in copyright, they indicate that a trademark is protected. But they don't mean the same thing.

TM means "trademarked," and it applies automatically when a mark is first put to use in the market—kind of like how copyright happens just by the author creating a work in fixed form. The TM gives notice to everyone that you claim this mark, and if they use it, you'll pitch a big fit. *But that's all it means*, because the trademark is not necessarily protectible in court unless it's been registered with the US Patent and Trademark Office.

That's what the **R** indicates: The mark has been registered, and if someone uses it, they will be sued and the trademark holder will very likely win, because the law provides protections for

---

[354] 15 USC § 1127

registered trademarks and punishments for their infringement.

Basically, those two symbols are similar to the ©: A © that's not registered just tells everyone you own a work and will fuss if they use it, but it lacks teeth. A © that's registered means you can exercise your statutory rights under law to protect your copyright. In trademark, the distinction between registered and unregistered is clearer, though, because the symbols tell us what's up.

Origins and Purpose

You'll recall that copyright law is established in the Constitution, to protect the rights of content creators and ensure that new, exciting ideas and content are both encouraged and made broadly available to encourage progress. Trademark's origins are not quite so lofty. Trademark is a law, but it's not in the Constitution—it's statutory, as mentioned previously, created by the Lanham Act in 1946.[355] That doesn't mean it's less "legal" than copyright, but it does mean that it's a newer concept, and its pedigree is a little less impressive.

The goal of copyright is to "promote the progress of the useful arts." The primary function of trademark is to protect commercial transactions and help ensure the fair running of an open, competitive, capitalist economy. Those are both very good things, but again they're a little less grand than copyright.

Trademark law covers both civil and criminal offenses. In both cases, it's intended to serve four important purposes:

1. **Protecting a mark-holder's intellectual property from theft or dilution.** "Counterfeiters can earn enormous profits by capitalizing on the reputations, development costs, and advertising efforts of honest manufacturers at little expense

---

[355] 15 USC §§ 1051 et seq.

to themselves."[356] Companies and creators put a lot of effort into making their products, and for someone to be able to swoop in and slap a creator's name on a shoddy imitation is just not right.
2. ***Protecting consumers from fraud.*** When consumers decide what goods to buy, they should be able to rely on a company's trademark and the quality that mark represents. Counterfeiting defrauds purchasers, who may be paying for brand-name quality but are getting a cheap knockoff. That's annoying if your Gucci handbag is fake; it can be deadly if your medication is falsely labeled. That's why "consumer confusion" is one of the main things courts look for in trademark cases: does the infringement confuse consumers into thinking a copy is as good as the real thing?
3. ***Protecting the safety of non-purchasing users.*** Trademarks aren't just for protecting manufacturers or creators and the people who buy their products: trademarks also protect non-buyers, too. For instance, if an aircraft manufacturer purchases counterfeit airplane parts for its 737, the safety of all the passengers who fly on that plane may be at risk. The passengers didn't buy the counterfeit parts, but the counterfeiter put them at risk all the same.
4. ***Enforcing market rules.*** Just like counterfeiting money or infringing copyright undermines the fundamental rules of a free and fair marketplace, counterfeiting trademarks weakens modern commercial systems.

Advantages of Registration

Like a copyright, there's no requirement that you register a trademark. But also like a copyright, there are distinct advantages to registration:

---

[356] Senate Report No. 98-526, at 4-5, reprinted in USC Cong. & Admin. News at 3630-31 (1984), quoted in House Report 109-68 (2005) on the Stop Counterfeiting in Manufactured Goods Act, which criminalized certain trademark offenses.

- Registered trademarks are listed in the US Patent & Trademark Office's database of registered and pending trademarks. That listing will show up when anyone searches the database for available marks, and serves as public notice that you own the mark.
- Registration creates a legal presumption that you are the trademark's owner. If you sue someone for infringing your mark, all you need to show in court is proof of registration, and you've made your case.
- Like copyright registration, registering a trademark give you the right to sue infringers in federal court.
- You are entitled to use the ® symbol.
- You can use your US registration to register your trademark in other countries, and you can share it with US Customs and Border Protection if you're concerned about copies being imported. [357]

Perhaps the biggest advantage of registering a trademark is incontestability. After your mark is registered and in use for five years, it becomes *incontestable*. That means the mark is automatically assumed to be valid, and if someone comes along and says it's theirs, or that they should be able to use it, they will lose. That's a pretty powerful thing. Once a properly registered trademark has been in use for 5 years, it can't be challenged in court.[358]

The only real limitation is that there's no incontestability for a generic trademark. This is a tricky one, because if a valid, non-generic trademark becomes generic—which happens a lot—it will lose not only its incontestability, but its trademark status altogether.

Let's a moment to look at that problem right now.

---

[357] US Patent & Trademark Office, "Why register your trademark?" https://www.uspto.gov/trademarks/basics/why-register-your-trademark
[358] 15 USC § 1065

THE ABERCROMBIE CATEGORIES

One of the central cases in trademark law is *Abercrombie & Fitch v Hunting World*.[359] Abercrombie & Fitch was founded in 1892, and for most of its existence was a sportswear retailer with a target audience of hunters and fishermen, boaters and campers.

We don't need to worry too much about the facts of the case, because it's the outcome we're interested in. Basically, in 1970, A&F sued another sporting goods store, Hunting World, for violating its trademark for the words "safari" and "mini-safari."[360]

The trial court found for Hunting World, and Abercrombie & Fitch appealed. Looking at both the Lanham Act and case law, the Second Circuit Court of Appeals identified four categories of trademark protection: generic, descriptive, suggestive, and arbitrary or fanciful. That's what's really important about this case: it established a new, organized way of addressing trademark.[361]

The appellate court found partly for Hunting World and partly for Abercrombie & Fitch, but that's not really important to us right now. What came out of *Abercrombie*, and why it's still cited all the time, is that it established the categories of trademark, which are still called the "four Abercrombie categories."

4 or 5?

First off, let's be clear about how many categories of trademark there really are. The *Abercrombie* court referred to "fanciful or arbitrary" marks as a single thing. Over time, those have been come to be treated as two different, if related, things. So in my mind, there are really five *Abercrombie* categories, even though

---

[359] *Abercrombie & Fitch Co. v. Hunting World, Inc.*, 537 F.2d 4 (2d Cir. 1976)
[360] *Id.*
[361] *Id.*

in law school everyone says four, because that's what the Abercrombie court said. So anyway, because there are really five categories, I'll say five here. They are:

1. **Fanciful**: composed of invented words.
2. **Arbitrary**: common words, but not connected to their characteristics.
3. **Suggestive**: suggests quality or some other characteristic.
4. **Descriptive**: A term is descriptive if it conveys an immediate idea of the ingredients, qualities or characteristics of the goods.
5. **Generic**: Identifies a product irrespective of its origin. Soap brand soap, for instance, or Computer brand computers. There is no legal protection for generic trademarks.[362]

OK so now let's look at each Abercrombie category in detail.

Fanciful Marks

Fanciful trademarks are made-up words invented for the single purpose of functioning as a trademark. They can be either words that don't mean anything in English, or archaic words that are out of common usage, or just nonsense words. A fanciful trademark is distinctive and only has a meaning when used in relation to a specific product. Because they're creative, unique, made-up words, fanciful marks are the strongest type of trademarks. For example, Exxon, Xerox, and Clorox are fanciful marks.

Arbitrary Marks

Arbitrary marks are words applied to specific goods or services that would otherwise not be associated with those words. That is, existing words or designs used *out of context* to represent a certain brand, service or item. Arbitrary marks are actual words

---

[362] *Id.*

that simply have nothing to do with the business they are applied to—for instance, Apple computers, Camel cigarettes, and Amazon online shopping. Unlike fanciful marks, they're real words, but because they don't have anything to do with the product they're attached to, they are used just like fanciful marks.

Suggestive Marks

The category of "suggestive" marks was spawned by the need to protect marks that were neither exactly descriptive on the one hand nor truly fanciful on the other. A term is suggestive if it requires imagination, thought, and perception to reach a conclusion as to the nature of goods. A suggestive trademark is entitled to registration without proof of a secondary meaning. Examples include Netflix, Coppertone, Tesla, and Best Buy.

Descriptive Marks

A mark is considered descriptive if it describes an ingredient, quality, characteristic, function, feature, purpose, or use of the specified goods or services.[363]

Descriptive marks can only be protected if they have acquired "secondary meaning" in the public mind that links the descriptive characteristic to a specific product. For instance, back in the olden days, there was a big phone book delivered to every home. It contained ads for local businesses, and it was printed on cheap yellow paper. Its name, "The Yellow Pages" was descriptive, but also linked to the specific phone book, and so protectable. Other examples include American Airlines, Hefty trash bags, and Premium crackers.

The Lanham Act forbids the registration of a mark which, when applied to the goods of the applicant, is "merely descriptive,"[364] it also provides that "nothing in this chapter shall prevent the

---

[363] Trademark Manual of Examining Procedure, § 1209.01(b) (2021)
[364] 15 USC § 1052

registration of a mark used by the applicant which has become distinctive of the applicant's goods in commerce."[365]

Generic Marks

A generic term is a trademark that has come to be understood over time to be the type of product or service that it represents. Under trademark law, terms that are generic or merely descriptive cannot become valid trademarks.

Way back in 1871, the Supreme Court said "Nor can a generic name, or a name merely descriptive of an article or its qualities, ingredients, or characteristics, be employed as a trademark and ... be entitled to legal protection."[366]

Words that are already in common usage can't be trademarked, which is good news for people who like to say "hello" or "okurr" without paying someone a royalty.

CASE STUDY In 2019, singer Cardi B attempted to trademark the word "OKURRR"[367] (a very specific, tongue-rolling, trilling way of saying "OK.") Sadly, the Patent and Trademark Office denied the application on the grounds that it was already a widely used term—in other words, generic. Specifically, the USPTO referred to its use by drag queen Ru Paul, and said "okurr" was a "commonplace term...used in the drag community and by celebrities as an alternate way of saying 'OK' or something that is said to affirm when someone is being put in their place."[368]

---

[365] *Id.*
[366] *Delaware & Hudson Canal Company v. Clark*, 80 US 311 (1871)
[367] Cardi B trademark application: https://tmsearch.uspto.gov/bin/showfield?f=doc&state=4801:2wthn4.2.1
[368] United States Patent and Trademark Office (USPTO) Office Action About Applicant's Trademark Application, US Application Serial No. 88335911 (2019); https://tmng-al.uspto.gov/resting2/api/casedoc/ts/cd/88335911/OOA20191113150839/1/webcontent

BECOMING GENERIC

The Lanham Act requires that any registered mark may be canceled if at any time it "becomes the common descriptive name of an article or substance."[369]

So here's what that means. Once upon a time, the word "aspirin" was a legally-protected trademark of Bayer pharmaceuticals. Over time, the word became the popular term applied to ANY salicylate non-steroidal anti-inflammatory drug. Same thing with the words "zipper" and "escalator," both of which were once trademarked and then lost their trademark status. That's the risk of a wildly successful trademark: a *specific* product can become so fixed in the public's mind with a *type* of product that people start using the trademark to refer to any product of that type. And that's when a mark becomes generic.

Here are some more examples of words that were once trademarked by someone, but that are generic today:

app   *teleprompter*
dry ice   *heroin*
laundromat   *linoleum*
trampoline   *videotape*
yo-yo   *zipper*

That list keeps growing all the time. It's ironic, because companies work very hard and spend a lot of money to make sure everyone knows their trademark, but once everyone knows it and it becomes associated with the kind of product it names, it becomes generic and loses its status.

So that's why you'll hear advertisements in which the announcer refers to "Kleenex brand facial tissues," for instance. The Kimberly-Clark company likes its trademark because it's

---

[369] 15 US Code § 1064

widely recognized, but they really, really want you to know that "Kleenex" isn't the tissue, it's the *name* of a particular kind of tissue. Let's look at some other trademarks (and their owners) that are at risk of becoming generic due to popular use:

- Adrenaline (Park-Davis)
- Astro-Turf (Monsanto)
- Band-Aid (J&J)
- Bubble Wrap (Sealed Air)
- Crock-Pot (Sunbeam)
- Dumpster (Dempster Bros.)
- Frisbee (Wham-O)
- Super Glue (Super Glue)
- Popsicle (Breyers)
- Realtor (National Association of Realtors)

I know I'm as guilty as anyone in genericizing some of these. When I say "adrenaline" I hardly ever put a little R in a circle after it in my mind. I will ask for a "band-aid" and be perfectly happy with any adhesive bandage. I cook with a slow-cooker that is not a Crock-pot, I throw trash in a bin that may or may not be a Dumpster, and I eat flavored ice on a stick that may not in fact be the Popsicle I call it.

Anyway, that's what that fourth element means: If your trademark becomes generic, it's no longer incontestable. If Kimberly Clark is unlucky, some day you might see a product called Puffs Brand Kleenex.

COLORS AND SMELLS

A number of companies have successfully trademarked colors associated with their brand:

- Louboutin red
- Coca-Cola red
- Wiffle-Ball yellow
- Cheerios yellow

- Barbie pink
- Pepto-Bismol pink
- T-Mobile magenta
- UPS brown
- John Deere green
- Tiffany blue

To successfully trademark a color, the color must have acquired a "secondary meaning" associated with the product or company it represents. That means that there's a popular association of the color with the product—that people looking down a store aisle will instantly recognize where the Barbie dolls are just by seeing the pink boxes, for instance.

Scents can also be trademarked, but in practice not many are because of the USPTO's rules for trademarking a smell. Essentially, a scent can be trademarked only if it "is used in a nonfunctional manner."[370] That means perfume and air fresheners can't be trademarked, because the scent is a functional part of the product itself.

So what scents can be trademarked? Scents that can be associated with a product, but aren't the product. For example, you might notice that when you walk into a Verizon store in any city, it will smell the same as all the other Verizon stores you've visited. That's because Verizon has trademarked "a flowery musk scent"[371] for its stores, as part of its brand identity.[372]

Another trademarked scent was successfully registered by Play-Doh, described as "a scent of a sweet, slightly musky, vanilla

---

[370] US Patent & Trademark Office, "Trademark Manual of Examining Procedure" § 1202.13   Scent, Fragrance, or Flavor (rev'd 2021)
[371] US Patent & Trademark Office, Trademark Status & Document Retrieval system, Reg. No. 4618936. (This mark expired in 2021, however, due to Verizon's failure to renew)
[372] This mark expired in 2021, however, due to Verizon's failure to renew.

fragrance, with slight overtones of cherry, combined with the smell of a salted, wheat-based dough."[373]

WHAT CAN'T BE TRADEMARKED

Any trademark that does what trademarks are supposed to do—distinguish specific goods or services from someone else's goods or services—will generally be approved for registration unless it:

- includes immoral, deceptive, libelous or scandalous words or images;
- Is misleading regarding the geographic origin of the goods or services;
- Includes the flag or coat of arms or other insignia of the United States, or of any state or municipality, or of any foreign country;
- Consists of a name, portrait, or signature identifying a particular living individual without their consent (or the name, signature, or portrait of a deceased President of the United States during the life of their surviving spouse); or
- Resembles another registered mark in a way that would cause confusion.[374]

TRADEMARK INFRINGEMENT LAWSUITS

To prevail in a lawsuit alleging trademark infringement, the plaintiff must show two things:

1. A valid and protectable mark; and
2. Defendant's use of the mark creates a likelihood of consumer confusion.

The court will apply a 2-prong test:

---

[373] US Patent & Trademark Office, Reg. No. 5467089
[374] 15 USC § 1052

1. Is the mark valid and distinct? and
2. Is there a likelihood of confusion? It bases that analysis on things like:
    - the strength of the mark;
    - the similarity between the two marks;
    - the similarity of the products or services;
    - use of the same retail outlets and purchasers;
    - the kinds of advertising media used;
    - the defendant's intent; and
    - any evidence of actual consumer confusion.

First, is the mark distinctive (this goes back to the *Abercrombie* categories)? A mark is distinctive if it's instantly recognizable as identifying a specific source, or if it is not inherently distinctive, but has acquired a "secondary meaning" in the public mind. That is, the public identifies the mark with a specific source. We use Apple a lot as an example, but it's a good one.

On its own, an "Apple" with a bite out of it is just someone else's piece of fruit. But sometimes it's a manufacturer of iPhones and computers and tablets and other stuff. The apple has acquired a secondary meaning in the eyes of the public, and is a distinctive trademark that a certain large tech company take great pains to protect.

ⒸASE STUDY Consider the Hershey Bar. It's a rectangular bar of chocolate divided into twelve equal segments in a four by three arrangement, with each segment scored around the edge and recessed with a raised border design.[375] If that sentence sounded weird, it's because it's from Hershey's trademark application describing their candy bar, which they tried to trademark back in 2012.

---

[375] US Patent & Trademark Office, *In re Hershey Chocolate and Confectionary Corporation*, Serial No. 77809223 (Trademark Trial and Appeal Board, 2012); https://ttabvue.uspto.gov/ttabvue/ttabvue-77809223-EXA-15.pdf

While Hershey's was ultimately successful, we did learn that a rectangular chocolate bar would be considered functional. And that a rectangular chocolate bar divided into twelve 4x3 segments would also be functional. But because Hershey bars also have the ornamental recess and raised border pattern, the Trademark Office's appeals board found it was distinctive and granted a trademark. But what that decision means is that other chocolate makers are absolutely allowed to manufacture rectangular chocolate bars divided into 4x3 scored segments; they just can't add that raised rounded border.[376]

 **So what do you take away from all this? Here are four key points to remember:**

1. Trademark identifies and distinguishes the source of the goods of one party from those of others, and can be used to protect things that copyright doesn't protect.
2. While copyright is in the Constitution, trademark is created by statute. Copyright's purpose is to "promote the progress of the useful arts," while the primary function of trademark is to protect commercial transactions.
3. There are five types of trademarks (or "Abercrombie Categories"). In descending order of strength they are: Fanciful, Arbitrary; Suggestive; Descriptive; and Generic.
4. A valid trademark can become generic and unprotected if it enters the public consciousness as a catch-all word for a whole type of product.

---

[376] *Id.*

Chapter 16

Introduction to Patents

Patents are a lot like copyrights, in many ways. Like copyright, patents are established in the Constitution—in fact, the same Article I, section 8: "Congress shall have power . . . to promote the progress of science and useful arts, by securing for limited times to authors and inventors the exclusive right to their respective writings and discoveries." Copyrights are for authors, and patents are for inventors.

Like copyrights, patents have been a part of American history for over two hundred years: From 1790 to 1849, patents were handled by the State Department. In 1849, the Patent Office left the State Department and became (for some reason) part of the Department of the Interior (which is generally concerned with forests, natural resources, and maintenance of federal land), and there it stayed for more than 125 years until Congress renamed it the US Patent and Trademark Office (USPTO) and moved it to the Commerce Department, where it lives today.[377]

Over the more than 230 years since its founding, the US Patent Office has issued more than 7.8 million patents, 7.2 million of

---

[377] USPTO, "General Information Concerning Patents," https://www.uspto.gov/patents/basics/general-information-patents

which were for original inventions.[378] Today, active US patents are worth over $3 trillion.[379]

WHAT ARE PATENTS?

Let's start with what *isn't* a patent, just to be clear. We've already said that patents are a lot like copyrights, but they're not the same. They're also not the same as trademarks.

A **copyright** protects original artistic, literary, or intellectually created works, such as novels, music, movies, software code, photographs, and paintings. A **trademark**, as we've seen, is a word, phrase, or design that identifies your goods or services, distinguishes them from other people's goods or services, or indicates the source of your goods or services.[380]

A **patent**, on the other hand, is an exclusive right granted for an invention or innovation. To be specific, patents protect processes or products that provide a new way of doing something or a new technical solution to a problem.[381]

In other words, as the patent statute puts it, "Whoever invents or discovers any new and useful process, machine, manufacture, or composition of matter, or any new and useful improvement thereof, may obtain a patent [for it]…"[382]

To obtain that patent, though, the inventor is required to disclose the technical and operational specifications of their invention in a patent application. The application is a public

---

[378] https://www.uspto.gov/web/offices/ac/ido/oeip/taf/brochure.htm
[379] ShareAmerica, "The high value of US patents," (April 2022) https://share.america.gov/high-value-of-us-patents/#:~:text=US%20patents%20are%20worth%20just,property%20(PDF%2C%20723KB).
[380] Adapted from USPTO, "General Information Concerning Patents," https://www.uspto.gov/patents/basics/general-information-patents
[381] *Id.*
[382] 35 US Code § 101 - Inventions patentable

disclosure, so others are able to learn details about the invention.

> *Just like anyone can read a copyrighted book, anyone can see the specifications and technical details of a patented invention. And like copyright, patent provides the patent-holder with specific, exclusive rights to protect their invention from being exploited by other people.*

A Negative Right

A patent is not the right to make, sell, or use your invention. It's the right to *prevent* other people from making, selling, or using your invention without your permission.[383]

It's right there in the statute: "the right to exclude others from making, using, offering for sale, or selling" your invention in the US.[384] The tricky part is that the responsibility for enforcing your patent—for "excluding others"—is entirely on the patent-holder. The USPTO doesn't offer any enforcement or legal support for inventors.

A Limited Period

Like a copyright, a patent's protection lasts only for a limited time. For copyright, as we've seen, the period is generally the life of the creator plus 70 years. A utility patent, on the other hand, offers protection for only 20 years, after which time others are free to reproduce, improve, and change the patented item.[385] The term of protection begins on the date the patent application is filed with the USPTO.

---

[383] WIPO, "Patents" https://www.wipo.int/patents/en/
[384] 35 US Code § 154(a)(1), "Contents and term of patent; provisional rights"
[385] 35 USC §154(a)(2), "Contents and term of patent; provisional rights"; 35 USC. §161, "Plant Patents"

That 20 year term isn't automatic, though. Maintenance fees[386] have to be paid to the USPTO at 3.5, 7.5 and 11.5 years from the date the patent is granted in order to keep the patent from expiring early.[387] The USPTO allows a six-month grace period for payment of maintenance fees. If the maintenance fee is not paid on time and the maintenance fee and surcharge are not paid during the grace period, the patent expires on the date the grace period ends.[388]

The USPTO does not issue reminders, bills, or notices that maintenance fees are due. Keeping track of that schedule is up to the patent-holder.

TYPES OF PATENTS

There are three types of patents: utility, design, and plant patents.

Utility Patents

Utility patents are granted to anyone who invents or discovers any new and useful process, machine, article of manufacture, or composition of matter, or any new and useful improvement of an existing invention or discovery.

Design Patents

Design patents are granted to anyone who invents a new, non-obvious, original, *ornamental* design for an article of manufacture. The design patent protects only the appearance of the design, but not any structural or functional features. Design

---

[386] Fees are adjusted by USPTO. Current fees, including maintenance fees, can be found on the USPTO website:
https://www.uspto.gov/learning-and-resources/fees-and-payment/uspto-fee-schedule
[387] 37 CFR §1.362(d)
[388] USPTO, "General Information Concerning Patents,"
https://www.uspto.gov/patents/basics/general-information-patents

patents are essentially decorative, but may also include such things as making a keyboard more ergonomic. The ergonomic add-on is considered "ornamental" to the patented keyboard, even though it does have a function.

Design patents offer a protective term of 15 years.

Plant Patents

Plant patents are granted to anyone who invents or discovers and reproduces any distinct and new variety of plant. The plant must be reproduced asexually—that is, in a way that doesn't involve simply sticking seeds in the ground—through rootings, cuttings, budding, or grafting.

To be eligible for a patent, a plant must be original and created— not simply something new found growing naturally in the forest or other non-cultivated area. However, a plant found in a cultivated area that is a hybrid or mutant of cultivated plants can be patented.

The term of a plant patent, like a utility patent, is 20 years from the date on which the application for the patent was filed.

WHAT CAN BE PATENTED

The answer to the question, "what can be patented?" is pretty easy: patents are only granted to inventions that are (1) new and (2) useful.[389] That includes the original "process, machine, manufacture, or composition of matter"[390] as well as unique improvements to it that are not immediately obvious.[391] For example, simply changing the color of a patented invention would not be a patentable improvement.

---

[389] 35 US Code § 101, Inventions patentable
[390] *Id.*
[391] *Id.*

Definitions

Let's break those categories down a little.

Process. A "process" is defined under the law as a series of actions or steps.[392] For example, Amazon's One-Click buying process, or the arrangement of machines in an assembly line.

Machine. A "machine" is a tangible, concrete thing made up of a combination of devices or parts, designed to do a specific task.[393] A bicycle is a machine, and so is an airplane engine.

Manufacture. A "manufacture" is anything that is created from raw materials. Examples include coated wires, plastic tubes, and, construction materials. What makes it novel is new ways of producing the article or the use of new raw or prepared materials.

Composition of Matter. Any combination of two or more substances, whether mechanically or chemically, constitutes a patentable "composition of matter."[394] That could include pharmaceuticals or processed foods or metal alloys.

Software

Interestingly, software can be protected by both copyright and patent. Copyright protects the code written by the programmer, and a patent will protect what the software does—usually a process.

WHAT CAN'T BE PATENTED

An invention cannot be patented if it was known or used by others before it was invented, or if it was patented or in public

---

[392] USPTO, "General Information Concerning Patents," https://www.uspto.gov/patents/basics/general-information-patents
[393] *Id.*
[394] *Id.*

use in the US or abroad more than a year before a patent was applied for.[395]

Abstract ideas, laws of nature, or natural phenomena cannot be patented.[396] For example, Einstein couldn't patent $E = mc^2$ and Newton couldn't have patented the law of gravity.[397] Literary, dramatic, musical or artistic works, while certainly protectable by copyright, cannot be patented, because the USPTO doesn't consider such works to be "useful." Similarly, a process or machine that doesn't actually do what its inventor claims would also not be considered "useful," and wouldn't be eligible for patent protection. And it's probably just as well that inventions used only for nuclear or atomic energy or weapons are not patentable.[398]

HOW WILL PEOPLE KNOW I HAVE A PATENT?

Unlike copyright, which uses the ©, or trademark's TM, there's no symbol that communicates that something is patented. Instead, a patented product needs to display one of two phrases to let people know the patent status.

Patent Pending

"Patent Pending" means just what it says: the inventor is letting the world know that they've filed the necessary paperwork and fees with the US Patent and Trademark Office. Typically, a patent may take up to two years to be granted, and often an inventor won't want to wait that long to begin marketing their invention. "Patent Pending" (or "Pat. Pend." or "Patent Applied For") lets anyone who may be tempted to copy something know that they can be sued once the patent is granted. At this point, though, there's no real protection provided: that only happens

---

[395] 35 US Code § 102, Conditions for patentability; novelty
[396] USPTO, "General Information Concerning Patents," https://www.uspto.gov/patents/basics/general-information-patents
[397] Diamond v. Chakrabarty, 447 US 303 (1980)
[398] 42 USC. 2181(a)

once the item is patented. It's actually against the law to claim that something is patented when it's not.[399]

Patent Reg.

Once a patent has been granted by the USPTO, the inventor can place "Patent Reg." or "Patent Registration" along with the registration number, on the product. Failure to mark the product as patented may result in the inventor being unable to recover damages for infringement.[400]

CASE STUDY In *Diamond v. Chakrabarty*,[401] the US Supreme Court was asked to decide whether genetically-modified organisms can be patented. Chakrabarty, a genetic engineer, had created a strain of bacteria that broke down crude oil. The bacteria would be very useful in cleaning up oil spills.

Chakrabarty applied for three patents: one for the process by which the new bacteria were created from an existing species; one for the chemical soup in which the bacteria lived (as a "composition of matter"); and one for the bacteria species itself. While the USPTO granted the first two patent applications, it refused to issue a patent for the bacteria, on the basis that "living things" were not patentable as "processes, machines, manufactures, or compositions of matter."

The decision was appealed to the Board of Patent Appeals , which agreed with the USPTO's decision. But the Court of Customs and Patent Appeals ruled in Chakrabarty's favor. The USPTO appealed to the Supreme Court, which also found in favor of Chakrabarty.

---

[399] 35 US Code § 292 - False marking. There's a $500 penalty for every false claim of patent.
[400] USPTO, "General Information Concerning Patents," https://www.uspto.gov/patents/basics/general-information-patents
[401] Diamond v. Chakrabarty, 447 US 303 (1980)

The Court wrote, "[Chakrabarty] has produced a new bacterium with markedly different characteristics from any found in nature and one having the potential for significant utility. His discovery is not nature's handiwork, but his own; accordingly it is patentable" as a composition of matter.[402]

 So what do you take away from all this? Here are four key points to remember:

1. Patents, like copyrights, are in the US Constitution.
2. To be considered patentable, an invention must be both new and useful.
3. Patents generally protect inventions for only 15 to 20 years.
4. Abstract ideas, laws of nature, natural phenomena, or literary, dramatic, or artistic works cannot be patented.

---

[402] *Id.*

About the Author

For over 30 years, Evan Butterfield, MA, JD, has been a publishing professional focused on explaining copyright law and applications to non-lawyer audiences. Evan received his MA in English from the University of Illinois-Urbana, and his JD from DePaul University in Chicago.

At Kaplan Professional Publishing, Evan became Publisher and VP of Product Development. While there, he wrote articles and gave regular formal presentations about copyright law to industry audiences of real estate agents, educators, and regulators.

At the IEEE Computer Society, Evan was Director of Products & Services, overseeing more than thirty magazines, scholarly journals and books on computer science, plus dozens of international conferences. At IEEE, Evan continued to focus on copyright and intellectual property, and helped lead the development of the association's licensing and open access policies. After retiring, Evan taught copyright and trademark classes for the Art Institute of Las Vegas, and since 2020, he created and has been teaching an online criminal intellectual property course at Arizona State University

Evan lives in Las Vegas, Nevada with his husband and cat, and is a creative person himself: he has been publishing and displaying his own odd photography for many years.

Want to Learn More?

Check out **www.copyrightforcreatives.com**, where you can access extra online features including

- *Copyright for Creatives* Updates
- *Copyright for Creatives* Blog
- Contact the author

You can email Evan your own copyright questions at

copyrightforcreatives@gmail.com

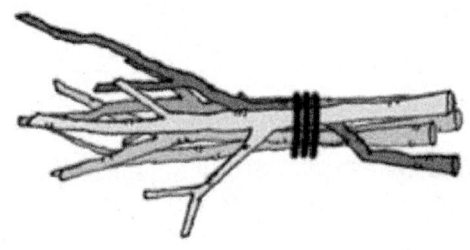

Printed in Great Britain
by Amazon